Northampt
Murder
Tales

Unfamiliar Cases and some Executions

Eric Jenkins

1998
CORDELIA

ISBN: 0 9522481 2 3

Northamptonshire Murder Tales:
Unfamiliar Cases and Some Executions.

Published in Great Britain 1998
by Cordelia (Eric Jenkins)
60 Newton Road, Rushden, Northamptonshire NN10 0HQ.

Catalogue Headings:
Murder: Case Studies
Northamptonshire
Capital Punishment
Courts: Assizes
Criminology

Also by Eric Jenkins:
Victorian Northamptonshire: The Early Years;
Workhouse Tales: True Stories of the Victorian Poor Law.

Printed by:
Allison Printers, Thrift Street, Wollaston, Nortamptonshire

INTRODUCTION

This collection of Northamptonshire homicides is not intended to duplicate or improve on anthologies that have been published by others. Readers will find these cases unfamiliar. Sources include contemporary broadsheets and press reports, court and legal records, scrapbooks, publications long out of print, and my own extensive files. Tribute must be paid to the valuable assistance of county librarians and archivists, and family reviewers.

ROAST HUSBAND (1329)

Clustered along the ancient trackway of Banbury Lane, southwest of Northampton, lie three small communities. Grimscote is only a mile from Pattishall along the old footpaths, and Cold Higham is in the middle.

Some time early in the fourteenth century, John fitz John, of Grimscote, had left his wife, Joan, and gone to live at Pattishall. The deserted wife had a number of sympathisers. Malcolm and Simon of Potcote were probably her relatives, as were John le Warde of Maidford, and Friar Robert of the Carmelite order who lodged at the monastic house attached to the church at Maidford.

Joan plotted vengeance. The men agreed to help her to kill John fitz John. A meeting with him would be arranged.

At that time, most cooking was done in communal ovens in the open air. At Cold High am, one such oven stood near to Stephen le Chaundeler's house. Joan prepared it and heated it up. Then she sent a girl, Iseult Sayere, to her husband in Pattishall to tell him that his wife wished to speak to him urgently. John came to her, at once, in Grimscote. Together, they walked slowly back along the footpath towards Pattishall, talking. They reached a spring at Cold Higham, called Mayneswell, and stood there in conversation for a time. They were only a furlong away from the oven. Eventually, Joan turned and walked home to Grimscote. John headed towards Pattishall, and walked by Stephen le Chaundeler's house. Malcolm, Simon, John le Warde and Brother Robert were lying in wait. They grabbed John and shoved him into the oven, alive. He was burnt to ashes.

Joan was held in custody until the Justices in Eyre arrived in Northampton in November 1329. The jurors of Towcester Hundred presented her case to be heard by the Court, and the Sheriff of the County brought her before Chief Justice, Sir Geoffrey Scrope. She pleaded Not Guilty, presumably on the ground that she had not actually done the deed, but the Towcester jurors found her guilty as charged. She was sentenced to be hanged. The Chief Justice, as might be expected, raised the matter of the culpability of the male accomplices. In the

1

room at Northampton Castle where the common pleas were held, the Justices discussed the case. Scrope said that Joan had been convicted "as principal", having plotted the killing and heated the oven. Aldborough, another Judge, said that if one engages another to kill someone, he would be considered a principal. There was no contradiction, but the jurors were asked about the accomplices. They stated that Malcolm, Simon and John le Warde were all dead. The Sheriff was directed to apprehend Friar Robert, but was unable to find him. An ordinary villager would have been easy to find because he would have been a member of a tithing, a village team, but this did not apply to one in holy orders. However, as one accused of felony, he was outlawed. There is no record of his capture.

THE HOLCOT MURDER (1871)

On Tuesday 30th May 1871, Richard Addington killed his wife, Mary. They lived with their two young children at the extreme south end of Holcot village, in a new cottage, one of five with doors opening into a courtyard. Addington, like all shoemakers, drew leather from the warehouse and worked at home, but he was over a week behind with his shoes. The inquest was held on the following morning at the Chequers Inn, before William Terry, Coroner. The jury was sworn and taken to view the body. On their return, Richard Addington was brought into the room by two senior police officers. He was a slightly built man, with prominent eyes and a face described as "careworn". Elizabeth Warren: I am a widow, residing at Milton [now Milton Malsor]. I knew Mary Addington. She was 37 or 38 years of age. T h e y had two children, the elder about five. I was visiting my sister, Mrs. Thompson, who lives opposite. About nine on Tuesday morning I saw Mrs Addington driving some ducks out of our yard. She had fed them, and drove them out with her apron. We all live in the same yard. Her husband also came out of the house and they went into the street. I next saw them coming along the yard together as if they were good friends. I don't think it was a quarter of an hour after I first saw them. I was sewing. I heard him say "Come, Mary. Come in." She replied: "I told you I won't come in." Her husband then whipped her up like a child, and carried her into the house and shut the door. She screamed and said she would not go in. In two minutes she opened the door, and I went to meet her. She said: "Oh, Mrs. Warren, my husband has cut my throat. I shall die." I heard her scream before that, and I thought he was hitting her. The place in her neck seemed to swell up, and in a moment, as she was coming to the door of my house, the blood spurted out of her neck, on to me. She was able to walk into my house. Her husband came in while I was looking at the wound. She said: "My dear husband, you have killed me. You have cut my throat. I shall die." He said: "I know you will, in a few minutes, and so shall I in a few hours." I looked at the wound, and he said: "That ain't the worst". He put his hand down her bowels and said: "There's the worst." She asked the Lord to forgive her. He said:

3

"Will you forgive me, Mary?" She said; "I will". I then went to look for someone to fetch the doctor. I went down the clubroom, and think several went... My sister said they had lived like two doves lately, till he went to the public house, and then he was always excitable and irritable. During the night before, I got up twice, because I heard words, and twice I saw him carry her into the house. She then stayed outside, and said she would not go in at all. When he had beer, I expect she was afraid of him, because she never dared go in.

Elizabeth Harris: I am the wife of Joseph Harris. I saw Mrs. Addington on Tuesday morning. Her husband was with her, standing talking, against the back door of their house. I live in the same yard. They did not appear to be quarrelling. I can't say whether he was sober or not. Afterwards I saw them from my window. They were watching some ducks on the pond which is across the road. I never saw them afterwards, till I heard a scream, when I was in my bedroom. I ran downstairs straight out into the yard. Richard Addington came out of his doorway, and said: "Betsy, I have cut her throat. You can go and look at her if you like." I said: "You never done such a cruel thing." He said: "I have, and she's a dead woman." When I looked in at the door, I saw blood on the side of the partition. I then went to inform the parish constable.

William Clark: I am the parish constable of Holcot. I saw the deceased and her husband in the Chequers. It might have been a little after ten. He had half a pint of beer, and drank part of it, and he gave his two children a little. I don't know whether he was intoxicated. He appeared to be sober. He went down the street in the direction of his house. Ten minutes after that, Elizabeth Harris came up to the Chequers and said: "Richard Addington has cut his wife's throat." I went immediately and found him sitting in Widow Thompson's house. He was sitting in one chair, and his wife in another. Two or three women were attending her. I told some of them to make haste and fetch the doctor, and I also sent for some brandy. They gave her a little to wet her lips. Her husband said: "Let me ask her to forgive me." He went down on his knees, and said; "Mary forgive me." She moved her lips, but I could hear nothing. I said: "Richard, what have you been doing?" He said; "I have done it, and I am glad I have, and I wish I had done myself." I took him in charge, and stayed with him till the doctor came. He never said what made him do it.

Susan Lillyman: I went down to Mrs. Thompson's house, where Mrs. Addington was sitting in a chair, and I attended upon her until she died. She was carried across to her own house by four men. I went with her, and I think she died about half an hour after. I helped Dr. Marshall when he arrived. When she was undressed, I saw two cuts in her stays, and two in her dress on the left side. The cuts corresponded with two in her chemise. I had known her for seven or eight years. I nursed her first baby. Last evening, I saw Richard Addington here at the Chequers, and I begged him to go home. He said; "Not yet." He had been drinking, or he would have gone home. When he was sober, he was a very good husband, but when in drink, he didn't know what he was doing. I believe he was inclined to be jealous. I have known no reason to make him jealous.

William Kitchen: I am a police constable, stationed at Walgrave. I received information about half past ten o'clock, yesterday morning, and I found the prisoner here, in the custody of the parish constable, William Clark, who handed him over to me. I said to him: "I apprehend you on a charge of attempting to murder your wife." She was not dead at that time. He said; "Yes, I know. I done it. I picked up a knife from my seat, and stabbed her with it. I left the knife in the house, and I only wish I had done myself at the same time." At his house afterwards, I found that his wife was dead. He said; "I hope she is at peace, and I shall soon be with her." On the road between Holcot and Moulton, while conveying him to Northampton, he said; "I hope they will hang me as soon as they possibly can, so that I can meet her again."

Francis Henry Marshall: I am a surgeon, residing at Moulton. I was sent for yesterday morning between ten and eleven o'clock... I found her in a dying state, from loss of blood. I endeavoured to give her some brandy, but she could not swallow. She was quite pulseless and insensible. I found a wound on the left side of the neck, about an inch and a half from the ear, under the angle of the jaw. It was not bleeding, but her clothes had been deluged with blood. I tore them and cut them open, and found two other wounds on the left side, a slight wound on the right side of the jaw, and also one on the index finger of the right hand, extending down to the bone. They were punctured and incised wounds.

This morning I have made a post mortem examination. I found, on the left side of the neck, a clean punctured wound an inch and a quarter in length, passing across and severing the upper part of the windpipe and blood vessels, close under the tongue to the rear side of the right jaw bone. The wound admitted a finger. I found on the left side of the body. a similar wound passing through the cartilege of the ribs to the cavity of the chest, which contained a considerable quantity of effused blood. About four inches below that wound was another similar one, passing into the cavity of the abdomen. There was a considerable quantity of extravasated blood in that cavity. The wounds were clean punctured as if made by the knife I have seen produced here. The wound into the chest and the one in the bowels would have been fatal, and that in the neck would most likely have been fatal. The body was well nourished and in a healthy condition.

After two minutes' deliberation, the jury found a verdict: "The deceased died from wounds wilfully done by Richard Addington." The Coroner made out a warrant for the committal of Richard Addington for trial.

On the next day, in a private examination room, Addington, in prison garb, was taken before three magistrates. When asked by the Chairman if he wished to be represented, Addington said: "I don't know anything about how it was, so I cannot say anything about it. I hope they'll speak the truth. I have done this deed and I wish to suffer for it."

The witnesses gave evidence similar to that heard at the inquest. Additional points are detailed in the following paragraphs. Addington wept and sighed throughout, covering his mouth with a handkerchief.

Susan Lillyman: ...When he was drinking, he would have nothing to eat for several days together. He did not know where he was or what he was doing. He was without sense at all. I have never heard him find fault with his wife, but I believe he was jealous of her. I never heard him accuse her of any improper conduct all the time I nursed her with two babies. He used to come home and lie down on the floor till morning, and then put on his hat and go out again. He never ate anything in the house till he got over the drink. He would be like that for several days together. During these times, I never saw him illtreat his wife. When I went to nurse Mrs. Addington with her little boy, now five years of age, Mr. Addington waited upon her and did everything in his power to make her comfortable. The last child was born at Northampton three years ago. If anything had been going on, I should have known. She always seemed cheerful. I passed the house and saw them both, almost every day since.

After Addington had been committed for trial at the next Assizes, one warder removed him to his cell.

At Northampton Summer Assizes, Richard Addington appeared before Sir John Barnard Byles in the Crown Court, on Wednesday and Thursday 12th and 13th July 1871, charged with the wilful murder of Mary Addington. The prosecution evidence was again similar, but Mr. Merewether, for the defence, cross examining, drew out some important extra facts.

William Clarke, parish constable: ...I have known him twentyfive years. I remember something about his being kicked by a horse. I believe he has the scar on his head, now. I remember that about three years ago he was acting rather strange. He made more than one false charge against different persons, for misconduct. They were not true. One was about myself, and there was not the slightest foundation for it...

David Cooke, landlord of the Chequers: ...I had to put him out of my house on the previous evening. He appeared rather strange. He said something about wanting a "cress". I could not understand what he wanted.

The Judge asked if the strangeness was caused by drink.

Cooke: I thought it was not the drink altogether.

F. H. Marshall, surgeon: ...I find, on turning to my book, I did attend the prisoner about twenty years ago, for an injury received by a kick from a horse. It was a scalp wound. He was well in about twelve days. I do not think much injury was done. It would be impossible to say whether there was any internal injury.

Walmsley Tarry: I am a shoemaker at Holcot, and a member of the friendly society there. The club was held on Whit Monday the day before, and the prisoner was there. I noticed he was strange before dinner. He got up before he had eaten. On the Tuesday morning, I saw him by the duck pond. He sat down on the grass. His wife came, and he said: "I shall leave the country". He said it quietly. His wife said he should go by himself. He said he would go as a single man. She was not angry.

John Barnett, shoemaker: ...When he came to the clubroom door, he said there was something he had seen which was not right. Several members asked him to explain, several times, but he couldn't. I went out with him for a walk in the afternoon. He said there were two or three complaints about shoes, and he asked me to take his wife and two children while he was gone...

George Faulkner: I was at the Chequers on WhitMonday evening. He was standing by the cellar door, and he said the landlord had got his wife. I asked him to go for a walk, to get him away from the place. He seemed very cool, and he was not drunk. I left him, but when I went back, he was standing there, watching the cellar door...

On Friday, the defence address to the jury, asked for a reduced verdict of manslaughter; or, if they believed he was of unsound mind, not guilty, whereupon he would be confined till Her Majesty's pleasure be known.

The Judge, in his summing up, could find no reason to reduce the charge, so the jury had to decide the state of Addington's mind. After a retirement of ten minutes, the jury returned with a verdict of "Guilty of Wilful Murder".

When asked if he had anything to say, Addington stared down and said nothing. The black cap was placed on the Judge's head, and he sentenced Richard Addington to death.

The villagers of Holcot organised a memorial to the Home Secretary, praying for a commutation of the sentence. A solicitor, Mr. White, carried it to the House of Commons on Monday, 24th of July, and in the absence of the Home Secretary, presented it to the Under Secretary. It set forth testimony of Addington's two brothers, confirming a plea of insanity, and it was endorsed by the Rector of

Holcot. There was also a report from Dr. Prichard, the principal of the Abington Abbey asylum (now St. Andrew's Hospital), whose opinion, based on many years' experience of mental aberration, was that at the time of the murder, Addington was not responsible for his actions.

By the following Sunday, the day before the execution, no acknowledgment had been received from the Home Office, and Dr. Prichard went to see Home Secretary Bruce. He had an hour with him at his home, but the Judge had made no recommendation for a reprieve, nor had the jury recommended mercy, so Mr. Bruce was not sympathetic. On the return journey, it occurred to Dr. Prichard that if he could obtain a memo. from some of the jury who tried the case (their names were openly in the press in those days) it might influence the Home Secretary. Knowing that the foreman of the jury lived at Towcester, he drove there in a carriage and pair, although it was past midnight. He could get to London by the 4 a.m. mail train from Blisworth, arriving at 6 a.m., get a reprieve from Mr. Bruce, and telegraph Northampton before 8 a.m.

At 2 a.m., in Towcester, he roused Mr. Adams, the foreman. Adams called up a fellow juryman, Brown, who lived nearby. Neither of them were willing to sign a memo. because they saw it as a lack of faith to their oath.

On Monday, 31st July, Richard Addington rose at 6 a.m. A few minutes before eight, the hangman, Calcraft, pinioned him and led him to the scaffold erected in an enclosed yard on the west side of the old County Gaol. Addington ascended without assistance, and placed himself over the drop. Calcraft placed a white hood over his head, and put the noose in place. The Chaplain read the burial service over the living man. When the bolt was withdrawn, death was instantaneous.

The bell of All Saints' Church tolled the funeral knell before and after. The black flag was hoisted over the main prison gate.

Several hundred people had gathered at the gate, well behaved.

This was the first execution in Northampton for nineteen years, and the first execution in the county town in private. Elizabeth Pinckard had been hanged in public in 1852. The body was interred in the precincts of the prison, six feet to the west of Mrs. Pinckard.

MIDNIGHT RAGE (1785)

William Howell and his wife had to leave the cottage they rented in Wellingborough when it was sold and the new owner demolished part of it. His wife met a casual acquaintance, Jane Garner, and told her they were looking for a room. "Trouble yourself no further", said Jane Garner. "Come and live with Elizabeth and me."

Howell's version of subsequent events was written for him in a letter and sent to "a gentleman" of Wellingborough.

"Jane and Elizabeth Garner seemed very well satisfied at our coming, and told me they had been illused by uncreditable men, and desired me to assist in keeping all disorderly men from their house. They also desired me to keep a stick by me... I found them to be two very bad girls, who kept bad hours, lurking in the corners of the streets, and encouraging drunken men and soldiers to come to their house; and behaved like the worst of prostitutes."

According to Howell, while he was away doing harvest work in Bedfordshire, Thomas Mee frequently came to the house in the middle of the night. If admittance was refused, he broke the door open. His behaviour was "riotous" and his swearing "wicked". Early in October 1785, Mee came to an arrangement with the Garner girls. "He would give them sixpence and a loaf of bread now and then." On Monday and Tuesday, 3rd and 4th October, Elizabeth let him in, and "they made a great disturbance in the house, so that I could get no rest."

Mee came again on Wednesday night, two and a half hours after Howell had gone to bed. "I bid him go away, telling him I could get no rest, for him. He refused, and abused me very much, and also challenged to fight me, saying let me come down... He was ready for me. I went down in a great passion and found him at the door, with something in his hand not lawful... I struck him once and he fell down." Howell said that he helped him up, and at his request wiped the dirt off his coat skirts, "there being no blood that came from him at that place." Howell refers to a statement by John Penderill "asserting that he heard my wife say that I should threaten Thomas Mee's life." He declared it to be false.

Mee did not survive the effects of the blow that Howell admitted striking, even though he went off down the yard unaided.

An inquest at Wellingborough on Monday 10th October 1785 heard that "Death was occasioned by a most violent blow upon the left side of his head and temple by a swingell". A swingell, more commonly spelt swingle, was a flail. Mee "languished in great agonies until Sunday the 9th, and then died." The inquest jury brought in a verdict of Wilful Murder by William Howell.

Howell made a fatal mistake in failing to attend the inquest. He had run away the previous day, on hearing of Mee's death. The inquest would have been his opportunity to make known his version of the incident, and the verdict could have been a different one. He gave himself up, and was taken to the Gaol at Northampton to await his trial.

Jane Garner gave evidence at the trial in March 1786. She had called down to Mee when he arrived on the night of 5th October, that she would come down and let him in. Whereupon, Howell, who was "greatly exasperated" at being disturbed, told her that if she did go down, he would "do for her and him too". Howell went down himself, "took up a threshingflail, and opened the door, where, meeting Mee, he gave him a violent blow on the head with this terrible weapon, which brought him to the ground, and left him in a kennel near the door."

He told the girl he believed he had done for him, and if he had a gun he would have shot him. The Court heard that Mee recovered sufficiently to crawl to a nearby house, where the occupants bathed the wound, and not thinking it serious, helped him to his father's house. The family had gone to bed, but the door was unlocked. He went upstairs to bed, having more consideration in regard to disturbing his own family, and lay "weltering in his blood" until morning. A surgeon was sent for, and his skull was found to be fractured.

The jury at the Assizes found Howell guilty as charged. The judge asked if he had anything to say. "I had no intention to murder him." The death sentence was imposed, and then Howells said: "I am not afraid to die!"

A servant who stole from his master, and a sheepstealer also received a death sentence at that Assizes, but the judge reprieved the latter before leaving town.

On Saturday morning, 11th March, Howell received the Sacrament, and between ten and eleven o'clock, was put in a cart and carried to the gallows. It was reported that two or three times he called for the cart to be driven faster, as the weather was very cold.

A penny broadsheet on sale after the hanging said that Howell, on arriving at the place of execution at the north end of the town, "acknowledged that he gave Mee the unfortunate blow which occasioned his death, but declared that he had no thoughts of committing murder." After some time spent in prayer, he was "launched into eternity; and from the motions of his body and legs, seemed to die very hard. After hanging the usual time, his body was cut down and delivered to the surgeons to be dissected."

THE KING OF DENMARK (1880)

Northampton people might sometimes wonder why Denmark Road is so named. No other country has this recognition in the town. A Victorian public house stood in St. Edmund's Road on the corner of Denmark Road. It was called The King of Denmark, and in August 1880 it was the scene of a sensational tragedy. Thomas Litchfield was the publican, and his brother George lived in the adjoining house.

An inquest was held on Thursday 5th August 1880 at Northampton Infirmary into the causes of the death of Amelia Litchfield, George's wife. The whole story is graphically told in the words of the witnesses.

David Adams: I am a shoefinisher. The deceased was my sister. She was 29, married to George Litchfield. He is a blocker [heelbuilder in a shoe factory]. On Tuesday morning, I met George in Bearward Street, and he asked me if I would go for a walk with him to try and find Amelia. She had been away from home all night. We went about, and then after my wife and I left him, we saw my sister Amelia in company with a man named Smith. My wife went into the Rose and Punchbowl with Mrs. Litchfield, to have a glass of beer, and I went to get George. We joined them, and George said to Amelia: "Let's be friendly and make it up." She said: "No, I shan't." I called for two more glasses of beer, but I was refused. I don't think we were drunk, but we were not sober. We had all had a glass or two. We went to the Black Lion. He again asked her to be friends, and she said: "I shan't". Now we were all the worse for drink, and went to my house, close on five o'clock. George asked his wife to go home with him, and she said she should not. Litchfield left us, and about eight o'clock, we went to their house in St. Edmund's Road. Smith was with us. Amelia asked George if he would have some fried fish, but he wouldn't. They weren't chatting, but I could see they weren't quarrelling. When my wife and I left, Smith also left. The Litchfields were at the door.

A juror asked why there was talk of making it up.

Adams: I hadn't seen them quarrelling, but she hadn't been home all night, and my brother in law was trying to be friendly.

Juror: Where had she been all night?

Adams: I don't know.

Juror: What became of Smith?

Adams: We left him at the corner of the street.

Anne Litchfield: I am the wife of Thomas Litchfield, publican of The King of Denmark. George is my brother-in-law, and he lives in the adjoining house. He came in to us twice, and then went out with his brother in law. I saw him come home in the evening. He beckoned his little child, Florence, and said: "Your mother is down at her brother's. You go to her, and stay until she comes home." He then told me he was going to bed. Later, his wife came along our passage with her brother, and asked me if I had seen George. I said: "He's gone to bed." She said: "He hasn't." I went upstairs and saw him lying across the bed with his boots on. She was the worse for drink. They all were.

Coroner, C. C. Becke: Were you sober?

Anne Litchfield: Oh, yes, sir. I had never been out. I had got my business to look after. Adams and his wife, and Smith, left the house together, and I heard nothing more until Mrs. Bates came in. She said: "Oh, Mrs. Litchfield, George has cut his wife's throat." Before I could get round the counter, Amelia Litchfield herself came up to the door with her throat cut. There were two men in the bar, and I said: "For God's sake, someone go to the Infirmary with her. [A short walk] She said my name, but never spoke again. The two men took her. I did not see George after that. I daren't go into their house by myself, but I sent for a policeman. I afterwards fainted away, and I don't remember any more.

Frances Bates: I live opposite the deceased. Whilst I was standing at my window, I saw Adams and his wife leave George and Amelia standing at their door. She snatched away from him, and said: "I shan't! You go in. Go to bed." She went towards the centre of the railings in front of the house. George followed her, and caught hold of her, trying to pull her away. No blows were struck, but I heard a noise as if he was trying to strangle her. He was leaning over her. I went out to them, and she ran towards me. I could then see that her throat was cut. Litchfield had gone into the house. I ran across to the public house to tell what I had seen, and she came in.

P.C. George Berry, Northampton Borough Police: On Tuesday evening, I was at home preparing to go out for night duty, when someone came to the door and said I was wanted up the street. I went to Lichfield's house, but I didn't see his wife. I found him in the livingroom, lying on the floor, face down. I lifted him up and I could see that his throat was cut. A razor lay open on the table. He wanted to go to the closet, but I said: "We must get you to the Infirmary." As we were going along, I said: "Whatever made you do this?" He replied: "It's all jealousy. She has not been behaving as she ought to have done towards me." He asked where his wife was, and I told him I thought she was at the Infirmary. He said: "I hope she's not dead."

A. H. Jones, M.B., House Surgeon at Northampton Infirmary: The deceased was brought in at halfpast nine. I met her at the door and examined the wound. Her throat had been cut from ear to ear. The bleeding had almost stopped, apparently from loss of blood. She was pulseless, and what little haemorrhage there was came from little veins in the neck. These had been severed, but not the great vessels. I stopped the bleeding. The cut was above the windpipe, across and extended into the gullet, almost to the spine. She died about twenty minutes after admission. Before she died, I saw George Litchfield. His throat was also cut, but the injury was superficial. No vessels of any consequence were cut. Whilst I attended him, he said: "If only she had acted fair to me, I shouldn't have done it." Next morning, when he was told of the death of his wife, he said: "I didn't mean to kill her." He is in my charge still, but in custody. He will not be able to appear for some time.

The jury brought in a verdict of Wilful Murder by George Litchfield.

Similar evidence was heard at the Winter Assizes, on 27th October 1880, before Lord Justice Baggalley. For the defence, the famous Montagu Williams, Q.C., put on a show of histrionics that made some impression on the jury, ending his performance as follows:

"I seek not to steal your minds away, but I do ask you as fathers and as husbands to put a merciful construction upon the acts of this man when you are judging of what the quality of the crime is he is guilty of, if he be guilty of crime at all. I don't know that I can do better than to pray that the all seeing Providence, from whom no secrets are hid, may guide your minds to a true and righteous judgment."

The jury found Litchfield guilty of manslaughter only. The Judge deferred sentence until the following day:

"The jury have taken a merciful view of your case and it is now my duty to pass a sentence consistent with the nature of the offence... That you inflicted the wounds which caused your wife's death, and that you intended to kill her cannot be doubted by anyone. If after brooding over the course of events you possessed yourself of a razor for the purpose of killing her, there would have been [no reason] to reduce the offence below that of murder. But it has been suggested that your wife's conduct led you to contemplate suicide, and it is further suggested that you got the razor for that purpose, but when your wife declined to go with you into the house, you, under a sudden impulse, attacked her and fatally wounded her. Which of those views is correct, you alone know. The jury gave you the benefit of the doubt. In giving effect to their verdict, I cannot forget the great sanctity that attaches to human life, and I cannot do otherwise than pass upon you a sentence of Penal Servitude for the term of Five Years."

The defence advocate, Montagu Williams recalled the case in his published reminiscences, "Leaves of a Life" (1890). In the space of ten years, he had forgotten the basic facts. It is amusing to spot the gaps in his memory. "A butcher [blocker] was charged with murdering his wife... He was about six and twenty years of age, and his wife was younger [older]... The subject of his jealousy was a sergeant in the Black Watch, a goodlooking and strapping fellow, home on furlough...

The butcher returned home one evening, and found his wife entertaining the soldier to supper. Wishing to avoid a scene, he said he was not hungry when his wife asked him to sit down to table... On reaching the bedroom he did not undress, but threw himself into a chair... He went downstairs, found the front door open, and passed into the street, where he found his wife talking to the sergeant... He snatched up a carving knife from the supper table... Running up to his wife, he plunged the knife through her heart, and she fell dead at his feet.

"At the trial I did my best to save him. The judge summed up somewhat for a conviction; but the jury adopting my view, acquitted him of murder and found him guilty of manslaughter. He was sentenced to twelve months' imprisonment [five years!]

"This was my only experience of Northampton, which is somewhat of a rough place. There was no robingroom in the Court, so we had to put on our warpaint in the hotel, passing to and fro in wig and gown. On returning to the hotel, I was followed by an enormous crowd of the butcher's sympathisers. Many of them insisted on shaking me by the hand, and I was almost torn to pieces. One individual slapped me on the back, and exclaimed: 'I say, gov'nor, if you come down here and preach, darned if I don't go regularly to church on Sundays!' "Such was my experience of a Northampton audience."

CHEAP LABOUR CHEAP LIFE (1780)

In the days of the parish workhouse, overseers of the poor had various ways of keeping their costs down. One was putting workhouse children out in apprenticeships. A pauper child apprenticed to a local tradesman was one less mouth to feed at the expense of the ratepayers.

Tom Cottingham, a Weldon boy, was ten years old when the parish put him out as apprentice in Kettering, with a weaver, William Parker. He did not survive the systematic ill treatment he received at the hands of Parker and his wife.

An unusual inquest was held in Kettering, in February 1780. So many witnesses were examined by Mr. Dexter, the Coroner, that three days passed before the verdict was delivered on 26th February. Unanimously, the jury declared that William Parker, of Kettering, weaver, and Catherine, his wife, were guilty of the wilful murder of Thomas Cottingham, their apprentice, by beating, starving, confining, chaining, imprisoning, and for want of necessary meat, drink, sustenance and support.

Parker absconded, but Catherine was committed to the County Gaol to await trial. A description of the missing murderer was published on 28th February:

"A MURDERER.

Fled from Justice, WILLIAM PARKER, of Kettering, Northamptonshire, Weaver, charged upon the Coroner's Inquest with the wilful Murder of Thomas Cottingham, his Apprentice.

The said William Parker is a thin Man, about 5 Feet 5 or 6 Inches high, wears his own dark lank Hair, of a sallow Complexion, and supposed to have had on, when he went away, a middle Drabcoloured Coat, or else a grey Coat, and red Waistcoat, and his Hat flapped before.

Whoever will secure the said William Parker, and give Notice to the Constables of Kettering aforesaid, shall receive FIVE GUINEAS Reward."

Within a week, Catherine Parker was executed. The Assizes opened in Northampton on the following Monday, and two centuries ago no legal prevarication was allowed to impede the case. On Thursday 4th March, along with a murderer from Moulton and a highwayman, she was sentenced to death.

On 6th March, the two murderers were hanged. The next Northampton Mercury reported that "their behaviour was very decent and becoming" Catherine Parker declared that her husband was innocent of the murder "for which I justly suffer."

William Parker was never caught.

HONEY BEER (1783)

Exactly three years after the disappearance of William Parker, another Northamptonshire man wanted for murder, went on the run.

On Saturday 15th March, 1783, Samuel Smith, Coroner, presided over an inquest, at Byfield, on view of the body of Sarah Bush. She had taken poison. Witnesses testified that she was "with child by one John Saul". On Sunday 2nd, she accompanied Saul to a hayrick, near Byfield. They sat down, and he produced a bottle which, he said, contained "honeybeer" (or metheglin). Into the drink, he had infused a quantity of mercury. The witnesses supposed that the purpose was to induce an abortion. Sarah Bush drank it, "but perceiving something disagreeable in the taste, attempted to vomit." Saul prevented this by holding her head up. The mercury had effects much worse than the one Saul wanted. Sarah Bush languished for twelve days, and "expired in the greatest agonies" on 14th March. The inquest jury brought in a verdict of "Wilful Murder by John Saul".

The parish constable issued the following advertisement:

"A MURDERER, ESCAPED from Justice, JOHN SAUL, of the Parish of BYFIELD, in the County of Northampton, by Trade a Cooper, (and sometimes works at the Bottlemaking and Bend Ware Branches) aged about 29, five feet eight or nine inches high, broad Face, has a rough Voice, dark brown Hair inclined to curl, dark Complexion, grey Eyes, and rather round shouldered. Had on a light mixed grey Coat and Waistcoat with Metal Buttons, Corduroy Breeches, round hat, and Plated Shoe Buckles (if not altered).

The said John Saul stands charged in the Coroner's Inquest, with the Wilful Murder of SARAH BUSH, of Byfield aforesaid.

Whoever will apprehend the said John Saul, and lodge him in any of His Majesty's Gaols, and give immediate Notice thereof to Richard Harris, Constable of Byfield aforesaid, shall receive the Sum of FOUR GUINEAS Reward.

Byfield, March 21, 1783."

The reward was never claimed.

ASSASSINATION OF THE SPEAKER (1450)

S ir William Tresham had been a knight of the shire (County M.P.) since 1423. He was Speaker of the House of Commons until the end of the Session in June 1450, and expected to be reelected Speaker in the next Session, in November 1450.

This was a period of lawlessness and violence associated with the rivalry between the two main royal houses, York and Lancaster: the early rumblings of the Wars of the Roses. Tresham was a Northamptonshire landowner with houses at Sywell, Rushton, Hannington and other places. He had connections with both Lancaster and York. He was Chancellor of the Duchy of Lancaster, but also an agent of the Duke of York.

On Wednesday 22nd September 1450, Tresham intended to ride from Sywell with his son, Thomas, to visit the Duke of York who had recently returned from Ireland. The previous day he received a visit from William King, who pretended to have business with the Duke, and asked permission to accompany Tresham. King was in fact, acting as jackal for others. His real purpose was to find out the timing and route of Tresham's journey.

Between midnight and six on Wednesday morning, 160 men, described as "misdoers and murderers", went to Thorpelands, on the Northampton Kettering road, and hid under a long hedge along the highway. When the Treshams approached it was still dark, but William King pointed out Sir William. A spear was driven through his body, and other deadly wounds inflicted on him, including a slashed throat. One version of this assassination says that Tresham's servants were following, half a mile behind, and heard his cries. They cut off each end of the spear in him, and carried him to Northampton. When the middle length was pulled out of him, he died.

It is possible to make various guesses as to the motive for this murder. Jack Cade's rebellion in Kent had recently been put down, and this may have been an attempt at a "copycat" operation by malcontents. The Duke of York had recently been declared a traitor, and this could have been an anti Yorkist demonstration. Some linked

21

Speaker Tresham to the death of the Duke of Suffolk in 1450. That Duke had been sent into exile, but was mysteriously murdered on board ship. Tresham's widow, Isabel, suggested that the motive for her husband's murder was simply a longstanding personal grudge, and she named Simon Norwych as chief suspect. Robbery was not a likely motive, although a large sum of money was taken by the assassins, together with a gold chain, a collar, a signet ring, other jewellery, and the horses. The son, Thomas Tresham was also attacked, wounded and robbed.

In a petition to King Henry VI, Isabel complained that the ringleaders were still at large. "Evan", the spearman who struck the fatal blow, she said, was seen daily, riding her late husband's horse, with a child following him on Thomas's horse. The killers had no fear of apprehension, and were at large in Northamptonshire, bragging about their part in the murder. The Sheriff of the County, she said, dared not have them arrested. Two coroners had conducted the inquest, and adjourned it, instructing the jury to make further enquiries before they reached a verdict. The jurymen had been threatened by the guilty men. "Upon payne of their lyfes, they should no verdict give."

MILITIA STORES MURDERS (1878)

The redbrick twin round towers of the Drill Hall in Clare Street, have been a familar Northampton landmark since 1859. In Victorian times, predating the Territorial Army, it was the Militia Stores. There, in 1878, a scrgcant of thc Militia shot dead two other sergeants. Why? When the inquest jury at the Town Hall, on Tuesday 3rd September 1878, viewed the bodies of Quarter Master Sergeant Brooks and Paymaster Sergeant Griffiths, the man charged with double murder was not present. He was Sergeant Patrick John Byrne. The Coroner, C. C. Becke, first called evidence relating to the death of QMS Brooks.

Thomas Alfred Brooks: I am a cabinetmaker. QMS John Brooks was my father. He would be 70 next birthday. He had been living at the Militia Stores, and had just left. He has been living with us at 131 Clare Street for a short time. We were expecting him home to dinner yesterday. We were waiting for him.

George Simmons: I am 13 years old. My father is Edward Simmons. We live at Number 6, Clare Street. Yesterday, between halfpast one and twenty minutes to two, I was at the window, overlooking the Militia Stores. We heard a shot fired, and we saw Mr. Brooks staggering down.

Coroner: Could you see where the shot came from?

Simmons: Yes, sir. It came from Mr. Byrne's gun. He had a gun in his hand, and smoke was coming from it. It looked as though it was pointed towards Mr. Brooks. He arranged the breech, and appeared to be reloading it, but I do not know where he got the cartridge from. Sergeant Griffiths ran down the steps, and saw Mr. Brooks. He made a rush towards Byrne, down the steps from the messroom. I thought he was going to take Byrne's rifle. As soon as Byrne saw Mr. Griffiths coming towards him, he lifted the gun up, and shot Griffiths' head off.

Coroner: How near was he?

Simmons: About seven or eight yards. The bullet hit him somewhere behind the ear, and he tumbled over. As soon as Byrne had shot him, he loaded his gun again, and went round the corner. I heard another shot about a couple of minutes after.

Charles Hill: I live at Number one, Militia Stores. I am a pupil teacher. Yesterday, about half past one or a little after, I was having my dinner. I heard two reports from a gun. I should think two minutes elapsed between the first and second reports. At first, I thought someone was shooting birds, but the second report caused me to alter my opinion. I ran out of the house, into the square, round the east side of the buildings. As I was going round, I met Sergeant Byrne. When he saw me, he used some expression. I don't know what the exact words were, but I heard him say, "I'll shoot you." I ran some seven or eight yards from him, and then lay down. I didn't speak, and after a few seconds, I heard the report of a gun... I found I was not hurt, and I got up and went to the back door of our house. I went to tell my father not to come out, but he was not in the kitchen. I went round to the front door, and about eight or nine yards from the door, I saw my father, in uniform, struggling with Byrne. My father holds the rank of Quarter Master Sergeant. He took the gun away from Byrne, and then went over into his house.

Coroner: Would he have passed the place where Sergeants Griffiths and Brooks were lying?

Hill: No, sir. They were shot in front of the building, and this took place at the back. I had not seen them at the time, and I did not know they were shot. Byrne sat down in a chair, and Sergeant Goss put the handcuffs on him.

Coroner: Did you notice Byrne's condition?

Hill: When I saw him, he was cool and collected.

Coroner: Did he say anything before he went into the house?

Hill: He did not go in. His things were outside, and he sat down on a chair. When Sergeant Goss went to handcuff him, he took a hammer up, and he was going to strike Goss. A sergeant got behind him and held his arms, and Goss then put the handcuffs on.

Coroner: Do you know of any quarrel or disagreement between Brooks and Griffiths and Byrne?

Hill: No, sir. I saw Byrne every day, and I saw Sergeant Brooks every day. I know Byrne was addicted to drink, and was very often intoxicated. Well lately, since the training.

Jesse Hill: I am Quarter Master Sergeant of the Northamptonshire Militia, and I live at Number one, Militia Stores. I was having my dinner in my own quarters. There is no messroom: it is simply a recreation room, a reading room. I heard the report of a gun. I took no notice of it at the time, because you will frequently hear someone shooting at birds. About two minutes afterwards, I heard a second report, at the far end of the building. It was so close to the building that I thought something must be seriously wrong, and so I got up from my dinner, and rushed out. In coming round the end of the building, I saw Sergeant Byrne with a rifle in his hand. That was the north end. Byrne was doing something with the breech of the gun, and I was under the impression that he was loading it. I at once closed with him. I wrestled with him, and got the rifle away from him. Women were shouting, and I heard a voice say: "He's shot him." I did not know at that time that anyone had been shot. but I thought that something was wrong. I said to Byrne: "For God's sake, what have you been doing?" Byrne replied: "Let me alone. They've turned me out of my house."

Coroner: Did he appear sober?

Hill: Quite, sir, and collected. Sergeant Forsyth came to my assistance, and after I had got the rife out of Byrne's hand, I caught him by his arms, and marched him across the square to his place, where he sat down. I left the rifle at my own house, and went to assist in handcuffing Byrne.

Coroner: Did you examine the rifle?

Hill: I did not, sir. The policeman came and took it away.

Coroner: Who was in charge of the rifles?

Hill: Every sergeant has a rifle of his own.

Coroner: Whilst you were handcuffing Byrne, did he make any remark?

Hill: Not in my presence, sir. Sergeant Goss came with a pair of handcuffs, and we put them on Byrne. He resisted. A few seconds after he was handcuffed, he asked for a drink of water. I went through the sergeant major's quarters, which lead to the front of the building, and there I saw Sergeant Griffiths lying outside, dead. I heard he had been shot, but I did not know why, or where it occurred. His scalp was completely gone, and his brain was lying about the ground.

Coroner: His scalp was completely blown off?

Hill: Yes, sir. I then went into the reading room, and saw QMS Brooks lying on the floor. He also was quite dead.

Coroner: From a gunshot wound.

Hill: Yes, sir. Somewhere in the region of the heart.

Coroner: Now can you tell me of any disagreement or quarrel between either Sergeant Brooks, or Griffiths, and Byrne?

Hill: Not to my knowledge, sir. All I know is that Sergeant Byrne was very negligent in his duties, and his conduct has been brought under the notice of the Commanding Officer on one or two occasions. One time, Sergeant Byrne was a considerable amount of cash short, and it was Sergeant Griffiths' job to point that out to the Commanding officer, but everything was settled satisfactorily afterwards, so far as the money was concerned. In consequence of his irregular behaviour, Byrne was ordered to resign the colours and quit the barracks; and Sergeant Dowley was coming to take possession of his quarters. Byrne would have to give up his quarters to Quartermaster Sergeant Brooks, and it would be Brooks' duty to hand them over to Sergeant Dowley.

Coroner: So Brooks had been there and was going to take over the quarters?

Hill: I was not present, but I heard so. I heard he made some remarks about the quarters being dirty, sir.

A rifle was produced, and Hill identified it as the one he had taken away from Byrne.

Captain Bowman: The Quartermaster Sergeant kept an account of the rifles, and his book has not been opened since his death.

Coroner: Who has charge of the ammunition?

Bowman: It is kept in the magazine, sir.

Coroner: Who has charge of the magazine?

Bowman: I have, sir. Byrne had some ammunition issued to him when he went through his course of musketry.

Coroner: Is there no check taken to see that all the cartridges served out are used, or returned to the magazine?

Bowman: We take it for granted that more cartridges are not asked for than are required. He might have had them for two or three years, for all I know, or he might have kept them after training. It would be possible to do it. We take it for granted, when practice is going on, that every man sends for the rounds of ammunition he requires, and the surplus, if any, should be returned to the stores

Dr. Thomas Farrell: I am surgeon major in charge of the Militia staff. I was sent for to the Militia Stores about halfpast one. I saw the body of QMS Brooks. He was dead, bleeding from the mouth, and I opened his coat and found a wound on the left breast, through the nipple. It was caused by a bullet. I saw the body of Sergeant Griffiths. His skull had been blown off, and his brains were protruding. I cannot suggest any other cause of death than a shot from a gun.

The Jury's verdict on the death of Brooks was given: Wilful Murder by Patrick John Byrne. The Coroner now called the evidence relating to Paymaster Sergeant Griffiths.

Robert Griffiths: I am an upholsterer, at Number nine, Militia Stores. The deceased was my father, Samuel Griffiths. He was 54. I came home about ten minutes past one, and saw Sergeant Byrne talking to Sergeant Painter. I know nothing of this occurence: I only heard the shots fired.

Sergeant Edward Potter: I am with the Northamptonshire and Rutland Militia. Yesterday, I was in the reading room, with Quarter Master Sergeant Brooks and Sergeant Byrne. They had a few words over quarters. The QMS said the quarters were dirty when they had to be given up by Byrne, and Byrne was arguing the point. He got up and said he would go and clean them. About ten minutes afterwards, the QMS said he was going to dinner. A few seconds after that I heard the report of a gun, and on looking through the window, I saw QMS Brooks on the ground. When I got to the door, Sergeant Griffiths was at the bottom of the steps. When he saw Brooks, he said: "Who ever has done this?" He then turned the corner of the tower, and then I saw Sergeant Byrne's rifle at the present, as though he was in the act of firing. I called out to Griffiths to come back, but I had hardly time to draw myself away, when the shot was fired, and Griffiths was on the floor.

Coroner: Have you any doubt as to who fired the shot?

Potter: No doubt at all, sir. When the shot was fired, I turned round, and Griffiths was down, with his skull shattered. I remained with him until someone came.

The Coroner called together the witnesses who had testified regarding the death of Brooks, and asked if the evidence they had given was also true in regard to Griffiths. They said it was. The jury's verdict on Griffiths was the same: Wilful Murder by Patrick John Byrne. In his absence, Byrne was committed for trial on the Coroner's warrant.

On the next day, 4th September, Byrne, in uniform, with sergeant's chevrons, was at the Town Hall, before the Mayor of Northampton (Thomas Tebbutt) and eight other magistrates. The Court was crowded, with many outside, unable to get in. The Mayor read the charge: "that you wilfully, feloniously, and with malice aforethought, killed and murdered John Brooks and Samuel Griffiths, by shooting at them, at the Militia Stores in Northampton, on the 2nd day of September, 1878".

Byrne was considerably agitated, and there was a "convulsive twitching of his mouth as if he were about to speak". The spectators leaned forward to listen, but no words came. After a long pause, he whispered to Detective Inspector Smith, who then asked on his behalf if he might be seated. This request was granted.

The witnesses were as at the inquest, plus one other. After the evidence of QMS Hill, Byrne was invited to ask questions.

Byrne: His statement is the most correct that is made against me today. In the month of July, I catered for the sergeants' mess, and between drinking, I made away with twentytwo pounds. Last month, I drank nearly as much because I got more ready cash from home, and on the morning this occurrence took place, I was turned out of my quarters. The place was taken over as satisfactory by the sergeant who took my quarters. The door was locked and I was turned out...

Peirce (one of the magistrates): I think you should be careful in what you say at present.

Byrne: No, no, sir. I won't tell any lies. His statement [pointing to Sergeant Hill] is the only straightforward one against me.

P.C. Holt (the only new witness): About halfpast one on Monday afternoon, I was on duty at the bottom of Great Russell Street, about a quarter of a mile from the Militia Stores. I heard the report of a gun in the direction of the Stores, and I went there. I saw the body of Sergeant Griffiths lying in the front yard, and I then went to the square at the back of the building, and saw the prisoner, who was handcuffed. I was apprised of the occurrence by Sergeants Tilley and Goss, and I then charged him with the wilful murder of Griffiths and Brooks. He did not reply to the charge, and I told him he would have to go with me. He said: "All right. I'll go." The rifle was afterwards given up to me, and I now produce it. In the breech I saw the case of a cartridge.

Byrne had no questions for the policeman. The Clerk of the Court read the depositions to him; then the charges. The Mayor cautioned him that any statement he might make would be taken down in writing and given in evidence at his trial, and that he was not bound to make any admission or confession. Byrne: I wish to defer my defence. I reserve my defence.

Clerk (Wickens): Have you any witnesses to call now?

Byrne: No, sir. I will call them at the trial.

Mayor: You stand committed for trial for murder at the next Assizes.

The committal had taken two and a half hours. The witnesses were bound over to appear at the Assizes. Byrne, "dejected" was taken to the Borough Gaol.

At the Winter Assizes for the Counties of Bedford, Northampton and Buckingham, at the Shire Hall, Bedford, on Saturday morning, 26th October, 1878, Patrick Byrne stood before Baron Huddleston, indicted for the murder of Samuel Griffiths. It was not necessary to prove that he also murdered Brooks. Witnesses, including the boy, testified as at the inquest. A new witness for the prosecution was

Major John Rawlins.

Rawlins: I am the Adjutant of the Northamptonshire and Rutland Militia. The prisoner was a colour sergeant up to the end of August. Until a little time before that, his conduct had given satisfaction. Then I was not satisfied with his accounts. The training ended on 8th of June. As colour sergeant, he had charge of some of the kits, and his work in regard to them was neglected. He was placed under arrest, and I investigated the charges against him. He should have been tried by courtmartial, but in recognition of his previous good character, I decided to demote him. I took away his colours, and he was then compelled to leave his quarters. I gave him notice to do so, and he was to leave at the end of August. Brooks was Quartermaster Sergeant and it would be his duty to take over Byrne's quarters.

Mr. Metcalfe, Q.C. (prosecuting): Will you explain why the prisoner had a rifle and ammunition.

Rawlins: Ball cartridge was served out to the permanent staff on the 16th of August, for rifle practice on the rifle range. Byrne was one of the permanent staff. I could not tell whether all the ball cartridge was used. The rifles were examined both before and after firing, and the cartridge bags are similarly examined, so that if any ammunition were unused, it could be returned to the magazine.

Mr. Buszard, Q.C. cross examining for the defence: Why was the responsibility left to the colour sergeant?

Rawlins: It is a matter of practice that the colour sergeant returns unused cartridge to the magazine. I never heard of any irregularity. Byrne has been in the Army for upwards of twenty years. A man does not get to be colour sergeant unless his conduct is good. The prisoner is wearing a good conduct medal at the present time.

Buszard: His want of accuracy was due to his habit of drinking to excess, was it not? Do you know that the prisoner owes a considerable amount, now, for drink at the canteen?

Rawlins: There are not considerable opportunities for drinking in the barracks. There is a canteen there, and Byrne had been caterer, being succeeded by Sergeant Potter. If anyone were seen in barracks under the influence of drink, the matter would be reported to me.

Byrne was not reported to me for drunkenness. He was short in his accounts, to the extent of about ten pounds, but "want of accuracy" was not due to his drinking. I do not know what he owes for drink at the canteen.

Sergeant Potter gave his inquest version of the shooting, and was then asked about Byrne's drinking.

Potter: I do not know that Byrne was drinking to excess. I have seen him come to the Stores, drunk, in a cab. I was succeeded as caterer by Colour Sergeant Goss, but when I was caterer, I don't think Byrne went into debt for drink above fourpence or sixpence a day. Altogether, he owed one pound, nine shillings, for drink.

QMS Jesse Hill, who had known Byrne for two years, said that he had been drinking freely during July, but not during August.

Buszard, in his defence address to the jury, made a forlorn attempt to get a reduction of the charge to manslaughter, suggesting that there was no "malice aforethought". If there had been a revenge motive, he said, the target would have been Major Rawlins, not the two victims.

The judge, in his summing up, left no room for a manslaughter verdict. "If a man is possessed of his proper faculties, and used a deadly weapon, and death ensued", that is murder. The jury came back with a Guilty verdict, and the Judge asked Byrne what he had to say for himself.

Byrne (in a clear, distinct voice): I am very sorry for it. I had been drinking in July and August. I am a married man with a wife and five children. I throw myself on the mercy of the Court.

Having assumed the black cap, Baron Huddleston, in a faltering and almost inaudible voice, delivered the sentence: Prisoner at the bar, Patrick John Byrne, you have been convicted upon evidence which can leave no doubt upon the mind of any person in the Court, that you are guilty of the crime of wilful murder, and it becomes my duty to pass upon you the last sentence of the law. You will be afforded that which you did not concede to either of your unhappy victims, time to make your peace with your Maker... The sentence is that you be taken from the place where you are, to the prison from whence you came, and that thence on the day appointed, you be taken to the place of execution, that you be there hanged by the neck until your body be dead, and that your body be cut down and buried within the precincts of the prison in which you shall be last confined. And may the Lord have mercy on your soul.

Byrne was hanged at Northampton Borough Gaol on Tuesday 12th November 1878, having received the last rites from the Roman Catholic chaplain. The drop was carried there from the County Gaol a few days previously. Marwood was the hangman.

A LIMPING KILLER ON THE SLOW TRAIN (1985)

When the 2102 train from Euston arrived in Birmingham on Wednesday, 20th March 1985, passengers pointed out to the guard that the floor of the second coach was smothered in blood. British Rail transport police took the coach out of use, and organised a thorough search of the main line from Birmingham towards Euston, using the illumination of a locomotive's headlights. At 2.30 a.m., the body of a woman was found lying between the tracks at Harlestone, three miles north of Northampton Station. Northamptonshire Police were then brought into the investigation. At Kettering General Hospital, a postmortem examination showed that the woman had been repeatedly stabbed. Marks in the bloodstains on the carriage floor showed that the victim had defended herself; that the assailant had been wearing baseball boots made in the Far East; and that he had a limp, proved by a dominant left foot impression. Detectives travelled on the same train from Euston on succeeding nights, interviewed passengers, and put together the description of a suspect.

Two postmen, who had been on Northampton station had seen a young man stepping from the second coach of the train. He apparently changed his mind and boarded the train again. He was unshaven, with long brown hair. He wore a grey shirt, brown corduroy jacket and dark coloured trousers with flared bottoms.

The police believed that the victim was still sitting in the train when it left Northampton. When the victim's empty handbag was found, robbery was assumed to have been the motive for the murder. A man travelled from the south coast to Northampton and identified the victim as his daughter, Janet Mary Maddocks, aged 35, a social worker who had resided in Birmingham.

Evidence from Rugby proved that the suspect had left the train there at 10.50 p.m., and had sat in the waiting room until boarding the "nightrider" InterCity express to Glasgow.

On Wednesday 27th March, Northamptonshire police staged a reconstruction of Janet Maddocks' last journey. It had been intended to put a policewoman on the train and video her, so that the film could be shown on televison sets on main line stations, inviting evidence from regular travellers. The plan was changed when a Northampton woman, who realised that her features resembled those of Janet Maddocks, displayed on police posters, offered herself in the role. The press were alerted to the reconstruction, and when it was staged on the 2102 train from Euston, it degenerated into a riot. The police intention had been for the second coach to remain empty except for the female stand-in and genuine regular passengers. Although forty police officers were participating in the operation, they were outnumbered by reporters, cameramen and television crews. There were fights between pressmen and detectives. One press photographer was dragged away by his hair. The stand-in was very frightened, and sat silently in the carriage until the train reached Northampton, where police escorted her away from the reporters who were scrambling to interview her.

Meanwhile, two detectives, searching, for five hours through 3,000 used rail tickets, found a bloodstained ticket issued in a Glasgow Social Services voucher scheme for a return journey from Glasgow to Milton Keynes (via Northampton). The voucher had been issued in the name of Jack Roy. That was the name of a boy who had travelled to Milton Keynes two days before the murder, to answer police bail for an alleged burglary.

At 6.15 p.m. on Thursday 28th March, Jack Roy, aged fifteen, was arrested at his father's house in Glasgow, carried by British Airways to London, and thence by police-van to Campbell Square Police Station in Northampton. The next day, a special sitting of Northampton Juvenile Court remanded him in custody.

Janet Maddocks had been separated from her husband, Peter. On the day of the murder, she had been to spend the day with him, in London, and give him birthday presents. They had been to a West End cinema to see the film: "A Passage to India". After a meal, she saw him to his train to King's Lynn, at Liverpool Street, and then took a taxi to Euston. By a miscalculation, she boarded the 2102 slow train to Birmingham instead of waiting for the InterCity express which would have overtaken it and arrived earlier. When the train reached

Northampton, her fellow passengers in the second coach had all alighted except for Jack Roy.

Roy, having pleaded Not Guilty, was tried before Mr. Justice Bush, at Northampton Crown Court, on 2nd December 1985. After all the evidence, and the closing arguments had been heard, the jury retired; but then a legal argument began. The judge called the jury back. "Circumstances have arisen in this case where it is impossible for us to go on with this trial", he said. "I shall discharge you from giving a verdict. There are legal reasons for this, and I do not intend to go into detail, because that could prejudice the case. It will have to be started afresh before a new judge and a new jury."

The retrial was at Birmingham Crown Court in mid January 1986. Desmond Fennell, Q.C., prosecuting, said that Roy had demanded money from Mrs. Maddocks, threatening her with a knife. When she refused, he stabbed her in the neck with such force that the thrust severed her spinal chord. He then stabbed her repeatedly in the lower abdomen, dragged her body through the carriage, and flung it from the train.

Dr. Peter Andrews, a Home Office pathologist, testified that blood found on the victim's clothes and handbag was the same type as that of Jack Roy. The cuts and bruises on the back of the victim's hands showed that she had tried to fend off the attack. Another Home Office forensic scientist, Dr. Michael Harris, confirmed that the footprints in the blood on the floor of the coach matched the soles of baseball boots found by the police in Roy's flat. A bone handled flick knife found there, was the murder weapon. Margaret Gillies, a cashier at a Glasgow amusement arcade, said that she took a bloodstained tenpound note from Roy two days after the murder. Scott Bryce, a young man who had travelled on the train from Rugby to Glasgow on the night of the murder, saw Roy. "We got talking, and I then noticed his clothes were covered in blood. I asked what had happened, and he said he had fallen through a window. Then he handed me ten pounds to buy beer and sandwiches. The journey took seven hours, and most of it he was asleep."

Joanna Fleming, Roy's father's girlfriend, told the Court: "I was the first to see him when he got back to Glasgow that night. His trousers were saturated with blood, and there were splashes on his jumper. He looked like death, and very frightened. There was so much blood, I asked him if he had murdered someone, but he said he had been attacked by three Asian men who tried to steal his cassette player in Milton Keynes".

Rudy Narayan, the barrister defending Roy, called Edward Clarke, a close friend of the accused boy, to say that they had both sniffed glue since they were 14. "There were also times when we would go up to the Gorbals and do some LSD together."

Narayan called Roy to give evidence. He admitted sniffing glue since the age of seven, and smoking cannabis since he was 12. For 18 months before his arrest, he had regularly taken LSD, at first one tablet every other day, and then two tablets two or three times a week. "I tried to buy 400 tablets of LSD for £350 while in Milton Keynes, but only managed to obtain two tablets". He took them both before boarding the train. "I can remember getting on the train and looking through the window at Northampton station, but nothing else. I suppose it must have been me who stabbed Mrs. Maddocks, but I cannot remember. All I could see were patterns and colours because of the LSD. The first thing I remember was seeing bloodstains on my trousers. At first I thought I was hallucinating."

Desmond Fennell, prosecuting Q.C.: This was in truth, a robbery that went tragically wrong. But you have lied because you cannot face the fact that you caused those horrible injuries to Mrs. Maddocks. The motive for the crime was that you wanted to take her money, and the evidence of LSD is simply an Afterthought.

Dr. Amil Aktar, a psychologist at Birmingham Special Drugs Abuse Centre, told the jury that Roy, just sixteen years old, from a disturbed background, and having been a glue and cocaine sniffer from a very young age, "was the perfect candidate for a very bad trip. He could have been driven temporarily insane by LSD". He said that it was one of the most powerful and dangerous known to man, and that a fraction of an ounce could "transport the taker into a bizarre or terrifying fantasy land".

Dr. Aktar, however, added that he had heard no evidence that Roy was high on drugs at the time of the crime. "If this had been the case, I would have expected him to have told people about it, because it is the most obvious excuse. But that has not happened".

After the defence address by Rudi Narayan, the jury retired for nearly four hours, and then found Roy guilty. His previous record then became known. It was extensive, with convictions that included three serious attacks on women.

Mr. Justice Otton: Jack Roy, this was an evil and callous killing. You are a danger to women. You will be detained until her Majesty's Pleasure be known.

On 14th August 1989, Jack Roy, in company with another young convicted murderer, escaped from the high security young offenders' prison at Dumfries. He was recaptured two days later.

DEATH AT NUMBER SEVEN SHAFT (1879)

When the railway was under construction from Kettering across the Welland Valley to Manton, George Hibbs was a subcontractor working on the tunnel at Gretton (later known as Corby tunnel).

To understand the circumstances that brought him before the Northampton Assizes, charged with murder, we must first look at the evidence heard at the inquest on the body of his wife, Harriett Elizabeth Hibbs, held at Corby, on 23rd January, 1879. Hibbs was already in custody, and had a Stamford solicitor watching the proceedings on his behalf.

Mary Jones: My husband is a labourer employed on the railway. I live in a hut at the top of the new railway tunnel, in the parish of Gretton. Mrs. Hibbs, the deceased, came to my hut about four o'clock on Monday afternoon, the 20th, and soon afterwards, her husband came in with a man named Linger. They stayed in my hut until about half past seven. She had two or three little drinks of gin, and her husband had three or four pints of beer, with Linger.

Coroner, J. T. Parker: Were she and her husband on friendly terms?
Mary Jones: They appeared to be. She asked him to go home. He said he wasn't ready, and she asked me to go with her. I went part of the way with her, with my boy, and I sent him to go the rest of the way with her. As I was returning home, I met Hibbs, and I said to him, "My little boy has gone down with her, and you will overtake them."

He made some reply which I did not understand.

Coroner: Were they drunk?
Mary Jones: She was perfectly sober, and appeared quite well. Hibbs was not drunk, but he was a little fresher than usual. She'd only had fourpence halfpenny worth of my gin.

Mary Jones's fourteen year old son corroborated his mother's evidence and continued her account.

William Jones: My mother sent me on a little further with Mrs. Hibbs, but when we reached Number Seven Shaft in the tunnel, I heard someone running behind. Hibbs overtook us. He made as if to strike at us, but he did not hit either of us. I was frightened and ran away. He didn't say anything, but when I had gone a short distance, I heard him say, "Go home, you beggar". I did not hear any blows struck, but I did hear Mrs. Hibbs call out "Oh dear!" two or three times.

Coroner: Had he knocked her down?

Jones: I did not see her on the ground. They seemed friendly when I had seen them at my mother's house.

Elizabeth Rowe: I live in a hut near Jones' house. At about half past eight on Monday evening, I heard a scream, as though a woman was in distress. I also heard two or three screams of "Murder!", and I heard a man say, "Get up". The screams came from the direction of Number Seven Shaft.

Thomas Lines: I am a labourer, employed by Lucas and Aird on the new railway. I saw Mrs. Hibbs going in the direction of her house with the boy Jones. I went down to Jones' hut, and I saw her husband there, but he left a few minutes afterwards. Shortly after that, I went home to my hut, number nineteen; and then I heard a woman scream out, five or six times. The sound came from the direction of Number Seven Shaft. I did not hear a man call out. The next morning, I went along the tramway with Police Sergeant Meadows, and near Number Seven Shaft, I saw some blood, and also the marks of a struggle. Mrs. Hibbs was not drunk, nor her husband, when I saw him, but he had drunk a good deal.

Henry Linger: I am a timekeeper, employed on the railway. I went to Jones' hut with Hibbs on Monday evening. I saw his wife there. They were on friendly terms. Hibbs only had two or three glasses of beer, and he was not drunk; nor was she.

Anne Elizabeth Hibbs: I am thirteen years old. I live at Number 19, Corby Wood Huts. Mrs. Harriett Hibbs was my mother. On Monday evening, I was left at home with my little brother. As my father and mother did not come home, we went out to look for them at about a quarter to ten. We went along the tramway, and when we reached Number Seven Shaft in the tunnel, we found Father and Mother. Mother was lying on the ground, and Father was kneeling over her, trying to help her up. I said, "What's the matter with Mother?" Father said, "Mrs. Jones has been giving her a deal of drink". We got her home. She walked part of the way, but she fell down several times, and Father then carried her; and he also fell down. When we got home, I undressed her, and she said, "That's a good girl, to get me to bed". We all went to bed. When I took a candle into the bedroom, Father said, "Put that candle out. Take it into the kitchen". I took it away and went to bed. I heard Mother snoring.

Coroner: Did you look at your Mother?

Anne Hibbs: I did not look at her face at all. About four o'clock in the morning, Father woke me up, and said, "Oh, Annie! I believe your mother is dead. Get up." He then went and fetched my grandmother, who lives at Seaton.

Coroner: Did you see your mother while your father was away?

Anne Hibbs: No, sir.

A juryman: Did your parents quarrel on that day? Did you see them take anything to drink?

Anne Hibbs: They were not in the habit of quarrelling. I went to Jones' hut with Mother in the afternoon, and I saw Mrs. Jones give her some drink. I also saw Father at Jones' hut, and he had some drink.

Police Sergeant Meadows: ...I visited the tramway near Number Seven Shaft on Thursday morning, and I saw marks of blood, as though a severe struggle had occurred there. I found two pieces of velvet belonging to the deceased, at the spot. I afterwards went to Hibbs' hut and asked to see the clothes worn by the deceased on Monday evening. They had been dried and folded up. I was present when Hibbs was taken into custody by Inspector Barwell. He said, "I don't know anything about it. I was drunk". I found the hat of the deceased under a trolley near Number Seven Shaft.

Dr. Greaves, of Weldon: I examined the body of the deceased on Tuesday morning, and I found her face, hands, arms and legs very much bruised, which might have been caused by blows or falls. I also found a slight wound behind the left ear. I made a post mortem examination that morning, and on removing the scalp, I found a small clot of extravasated blood behind the ear. On taking off the skull and removing the brain, I found another small clot under the membranes on the right side. The body appeared to be healthy except that the liver was a little inclined to be fatty. The extravasation of blood produced death, and it might have been caused by apoplexy, or by a fall or a blow. No sharp instrument had been used, but the extravasation of blood might have been caused by a heavy blow with a fist.

The jury retired and consulted privately for half an hour. The verdict was "Manslaughter", and the Coroner committed Hibbs for trial. When Hibbs was told of the verdict he said: "I liked her too much to injure her."

By Thursday, 30th January 1879, when George Hibbs was taken before a Special Petty Sesional Court, the charge had been amended to "wilful murder of his wife, Harriet Hibbs". At the three hour hearing, Mary Jones and her son William gave evidence as at the inquest. Anne Hibbs gave similar evidence, but added some new detail. "Mother took drink on two occasions during the afternoon of the 20th: on the way from our own hut to Mrs. Jones' hut, and also when she went into Mrs. Jones' bedroom. She had three tots of gin there".

A small tumbler was produced in Court.

Anne Hibbs: Yes, a glass like that was about three parts full each time. Two tots were given to her by Mrs. Jones. The third was paid for out of a sovereign which she gave to Mrs. Jones. Mrs. Jones kept her company with a drink, and that was also paid for out of the sovereign. Mother suffered from fits, and when she was having a fit, she would fight and scream very violently. She was always most likely to have a fit when she was the worse for liquor.

The mother of the accused gave evidence.

Mrs. Hibbs: I am the wife of Isaac Hibbs, and mother of George Hibbs. My son came about half past five on the Tuesday morning, to my house at Seaton, saying he thought his wife was dead, and asking me to go back with him to see her. When we arrived at Corby Wood Huts, about half past seven, I found my son's wife dead in her bed. I pulled a cloth off her face, and I noticed there were bruises on her. I did not call anyone in at that time, but the police arrived very shortly after I arrived. My son told me that he and his wife had both had a good deal of drink the previous night. I have always lived near to my son. He and his father, as a rule, are engaged on work under the same contractor. I knew him to be a very affectionate husband. His wife was slightly addicted to drink, and I had heard of her having fits, but I never saw her suffer from one.

The police and medical evidence was as at the inquest. Hibbs was represented by the same Stamford solicitor, English. He addressed the one magistrate who presided: "No evidence whatever has been brought forward to substantiate the capital charge of wilful murder against my client, and I therefore ask that he might be put on trial for manslaughter only".

The application had no effect, and Hibbs was sent for trial at the Assizes on the murder charge.

He was brought up before Sir Robert Lush, at the Northampton Spring Assizes on Wednesday, 23rd April, 1879.

Mary Jones, of Hut Number One, Gretton, added some new information to her earlier evidence. "Mrs. Hibbs came with her daughter to my hut. Shortly before five o'clock she got into a trap belonging to Mr. Brown. Hibbs began to grumble about that, upon which, she got out again and came back into the hut with her husband. She was there until about half past seven. There was no quarrel, except that Hibbs threw his hat at her. She was sober and in good health, but Hibbs was not sober. He had three or four pints, with Linger.

Etherington Smith, representing Hibbs, had no intention of letting that pass. Under his cross examination, Mary Jones went into more detail. There had been five other men in her hut besides Hibbs. Hibbs and Linger had been served with a pint of beer each at two o'clock, and another at four.

The boy William Jones repeated his story, and Elizabeth Rowe told of the shriek she heard as she sat in her hut.

Thomas Lines, a railway navvy: ...I was in Jones' hut, with five other men. I stayed twenty minutes, and then went along the tramway.

As I was coming back, I met Mrs. Jones, her son, and Mrs. Hibbs. I stopped and spoke to them. At Jones' hut, Hibbs was still there. I went off with Linger to our lodgings. About eight o'clock, I went out to get some water. I heard screams, from a female, loud at first, then fainter. Next morning, I went with the constables to Number Seven Shaft. We saw blood, and marks, as if someone had been dragged along the ground for several yards.

Henry Linger's evidence ended with an additional recollection.

He had offered to go home with Hibbs, but Hibbs had said, "No. I don't want anyone".

Annie Hibbs: ...Mother and I were going to ride home in Mr. Brown's cart, but Father came up, and Mother got out of the cart. I went on...

When she reached the part of her evidence describing how Hibbs had woken her: "Get up, Annie. I believe your mother is dead", the girl broke down in tears. This greatly affected Hibbs, in the dock.
Etherington Smith, cross examining: Exactly what had you seen your mother drink? Was she drunk?

Annie Hibbs: She had a pint of beer before she left home, and another at Mrs. Spears', and three drops of gin at Mrs. Jones'. She paid for two glasses of gin at Mrs. Jones' with a sovereign. She fell down on the tramway several times. I knew she was drunk as soon as I saw her. She was often drunk. She was epileptic, and fits came on when she had been drinking. She fell across the fence several times.

Sergeant Meadows repeated his evidence of examining the blood and marks between the tramway and the fence at Number Seven Shaft.

P.C. Jesse Fennimore: ...I found the hat [produced] close to Number Seven Shaft, under a trolley which had been overturned.

There was a shock when the pathological evidence was called. At the inquest, Dr. Greaves of Weldon had supplied the post mortem details. Two other medical men were at the trial. First, Dr. Bayley, of St. Andrew's Hospital, Duston, told the Court: "Dr. Greaves is under my care, and completely insane." Dr. Greaves' depositions were read out, and then a surgeon from Great Easton, Mr. Duke, confirmed that

43

their contents were accurate, adding his own opinion: "The blood clot found on the brain of Harriett Elizabeth Hibbs might have been caused by a fall, or by a blow".

Judge: This evidence bears out the fact that the deceased might have met with her death through the injuries she received by falling down. The prosecution has failed, I think, to substantiate the charge of wilful murder.

Mr. Jacques (leading the prosecution): After that expression from your Lordship, I think I ought to withdraw from the prosecution.

Judge to the Jury: If you think proper, we might hear from the Counsel for the Defence.

The Jury conferred for a few minutes.

Foreman: Our opinion is that the evidence has failed to show that the deceased met her death at the hands of the prisoner.

Judge: I quite concur in that verdict, gentlemen. Let the prisoner be discharged.

Before leaving the dock, George Hibbs said: "Many thanks, your Lordship and gentlemen."

A crowd of his friends congregated outside the gaol, adjoining the Sessions House where the trial had taken place. They were disappointed. Hibbs was quietly released through a private door.

RESISTING ARREST (1559)

When Elizabeth I came to the throne in 1558, religious divisions were a major problem. A renewed Act of Supremacy gave her power over the Church, and a clause in it set up a Court of High Commission to deal with heretics and offenders against Church law. John Simpson was reported for religious misdemeanours, and the Commissioners issued a warrant "for attaching and arresting the body of John Simpson, of the parish of Alderton in the County of Northampton" so that he might be brought before the Court. The warrant came to the constable of Alderton, Richard Butler, who deputised another villager, William Johnson to assist in the arrest.

What happened next is told by a contemporary lawyer, "W. Huntley, Esquire" who took an interest in the case. They "came to a widdowes house, where Simpson was, at eight o'clock at night." They found the doors open, walked in, found Simpson, and read the warrant to him. Simpson refused to be taken into custody, and there was a struggle. A loaded pistol was within reach. It is not clear whether this was carried by the law officer, or less likely, that it happened to be lying about in the widow's house. Simpson grabbed it, and shot William Johnson, who fell dead.

Simpson was taken before the Northampton Assizes, charged with "wilfull murther". When the case was heard, a great legal argument took place. The authority of the Commissioners' warrant was challenged. If it were not valid, the constable had no lawful authority to arrest Simpson, who was simply defending himself against improper action. If this argument was sustained, the most that Simpson could be charged with was manslaughter.

Huntley says that this matter was of such "great weight" that the case was deferred until the next assizes. "All the judges of England" went into conference. By the words of their Commission, the religious commissioners had power given to them to "attach and arrest offender by Purcevant or Warrant". However, the words of the Statute, I Eliz.cII, which set up the Commission, gave them no such authority. Therefore there had been no lawful power to arrest

Simpson. The Commission should have proceeded against him by means of a caution, or some other "ecclesiastical process". The constable's warrant was "void".

At the next Assizes, John Simpson was again before the Court. When the charge was read out, the jury was directed by the Court to find him not guilty of wilful murder, and he was acquitted.

MURDER AT NEW HALL FARM (1883)

In 1882, George Bland, a 23 year old porter at a wine merchant's in the Drapery, at Northampton, met Mary Miller, of Hulcote near Towcester. They married in July at the parish church of Easton Neston, and lived in lodgings near Northampton Racecourse. Within a month, they moved to George's home village of Clipston, where George did harvest work. One week before Christmas 1882, the Bailiff of Grange Farm, on the Clifden Estate at Naseby, offered George fulltime work and a tied cottage. They moved into the little whitewashed cottage just as the farm's name was changed to New Hall Farm.

During the early part of 1883, George became slightly eccentric. Although his work was always performed properly, he talked of suicide, and on 3rd April, he told George Pratt, his foreman, that he was going to look for work some distance away. During the days following, he was rambling about the district, seemingly doing nothing. Because of this, Mary left him and went home to Hulcote. George followed her there, and persuaded her to return to the Naseby cottage, with her mother to keep her company, on Friday, 13th. On the following Sunday, he went to George Pratt and begged for his job back. He was reemployed, and promised to look after his home better, and make amends.

All went well during the next week. On Thursday night, he worked late, helping George Pratt until ten. Mary spent the evening with Mrs. Pratt at the farmhouse, and they all had supper together before the Blands returned to their cottage. Nothing more was heard of them that night. Because George had worked late, George Pratt was not surprised when he did not come to work next morning at six, his usual time. At halfpast seven, Pratt and another labourer, Ringrose, went to knock him up. There was no response when they knocked the cottage door. They found it surprising that the front door was locked and no key was in the lock. With Bland's eccentricities in mind, they suspected something to be wrong. They took a ladder from a nearby rick, and put it up to the bedroom window. There was no curtain, and they could see Mary Bland lying on the floor. They were able to open the window and get in. Mary was in her nightdress. Her throat had been cut.

George Bland was absent. Pratt sent Ringrose to bring the village constable, P.C. Davies. On the kitchen table, immediately opposite the door to the stairs, was a blackhandled dinner knife, not sharpened, but much stained with blood. So much blood had flowed from Mary's wound, that it was seeping through the ceiling of the downstairs room. The farm workers and the policeman thoroughly searched the farm, fields and pools without any sign of Bland. Telegrams were sent to the police in all neighbouring districts, describing George Bland as "24 years of age, five feet, nine inches tall, slim, with dark features."

Naseby village was scoured, but although the news of the death of Mary Bland had spread, no information on George's whereabouts was received by the police. A constable was sent on the train to Leicester, to walk back, in the hope of meeting George on the way. A detective inspector travelled to Nottingham, and another to Leicester, to ask for the help of other county forces in the search for George Bland. Arrangements were made for police officers to stand guard at the cottage during the coming night, in case Bland decided to return.

Meanwhile, information of Bland's movements was coming to the police. At 6.30 a.m., he had been at Kelmarsh, calling on his uncle, John Mutton, to ask for money. There had been previous loans, so he was refused. Fifteen minutes later, he was at Kelmarsh railway station, where he engaged in a scuffle with his cousin Samuel Jarman. A train was seen approaching, and Bland threw his body across the track in front of it. The driver managed to stop the train before it reached him. Bland went on to Oxenden and contacted another cousin, Harry Bland, and they went into a publichouse. While drinking together, George said to Harry: "I have done it, Harry. I shall go to Market Harborough to pay my club, and then I shall drown myself."

When the Leicestershire Police joined the hunt, enquiries were made in the villages around Market Harborough. A constable was told of a new dairyman taken on at a farm at Tur Langton. At 5 p.m. he found Bland, milking the cows. He said that his name was Chester, and denied that he was George Bland. There were bloodstains on his clothing, and he was arrested.

The inquest on view of the body of Mary Ann Bland was held on Saturday afternoon, 21st April, at Mrs. White's Royal Oak Inn, at Naseby, before W. Terry, Coroner.

George Pratt: I am foreman to Mr. John Everard, the Bailiff of the Estate. (He gave evidence of discovering Mary's body). Bland was generally a sober man, but seemed strange at times. On Thursday afternoon, he talked to me about religious subjects, and he told me that he thought he was really and truly a lost man... I had no idea at that time that he meant to do anything wrong. His wife left him about a fortnight ago, and went home to her parents at Hulcote. She went away because Bland did not seem to think of their home. A week ago they both returned, together with her mother, and Bland said he was sorry for what had taken place.

Kate Pratt: I am the wife of the last witness. Mary Bland was at my house the evening before she died, but nothing occurred to lead me to think there was any unpleasantness between the couple. I have heard that she was going home to her mother again, but she told me she was not going. When they both went home on Thursday night, they were friendly.

A juryman: Was Bland jealous of his wife?

Kate Pratt: I have heard that he was a jealous man, and his father before him, but I am sure that there was no occasion for it. She was a very quiet woman. I never heard Bland say anything disrespectful of his wife.

P.C. Davies: ...About half past eight yesterday morning, from information received, I went to a cottage on the New Hall Farm, occupied by George Bland. In the bedroom, I saw the deceased lying on her back on the floor, in a pool of blood. She was quite dead, and her throat had been cut. She had on her night clothing. A pillow partly covered with blood, was at her feet, and it appeared to have been used to place over her mouth. One of the sheets of the bed was also drawn down, and was spotted with blood. It had marks of blood on it, as if some person had wiped their fingers on it. On making an examination of the kitchen, I found a table knife covered with blood, quite wet. There was also a mark of blood where the knife had lain. In the pantry I found a tin bowl full of water, which appeared as if blood had been washed off someone's hands. I also found a piece of rope made into a noose on the top of a box in the bedroom.

James Craig: I am a surgeon, assistant to Mr. Headley of Welford. I saw the body of the deceased, about noon, yesterday. The cause of death was undoubtedly the haemorrhage from the wound in the throat. There was but little indication of a struggle. The deceased appeared to be enceinte. [Pregnant]

Superintendent Botterill: I am with the Northamptonshire County Constabulary, stationed at Kettering. On receiving information of the murder, I visited the house at Naseby, and found that the husband of the deceased had absconded, and was suspected of murder. I traced the man to Kelmarsh and Oxenden. I was informed that the man was seen to lay his head on the railway metals near Kelmarsh station. The engine driver saw the man on the line, however, and managed to stop the train in time. Bland then got up and ran away. He was subsequently captured by Sergeant Collier of the Leicestershire Constabulary at Tur Langton, and taken to Little Bowden Police Station. Blood was found on the cuffs and front of the man's shirt, and also under his finger nails. This morning I charged him with the murder of his wife. He replied: "My wife. I know nothing about it. I have lost my memory."

The jury found a verdict of "Wilful Murder by George James Bland". The Coroner made out a commital warrant.

On the second day of the Northampton Summer Assizes, Tuesday, 10th July 1883, George James Bland was brought up before Baron Huddleston. Mr. Sills, introducing the case for the prosecution, said that although the evidence that Bland killed his wife was clear, the issue demanding the attention of the jury was the state of his mind at the time. If they believed that he was insane, they would find him not guilty on the ground of insanity. "Evidence will, however, be called, to show that the prisoner, although perhaps not of strong mind, was sane enough to understand that what he was doing at the time was wrong against the law. His subsequent actions will also tend to show that he was sane."

He called George Pratt, who repeated his inquest evidence. The Judge asked him about Bland's manner.

Pratt: He seemed dull, and shirked his work.

Samuel Jarman: I am a labourer, and I reside at Clipston. I am in the employ of the London and NorthWestern Railway Company. George Bland is my cousin. On the morning of the 20th of April, I was at work near Kelmarsh Station, when he came to me, about a quarter to seven. A man named John Mutton was working with me, and he asked George if he was out of work. He didn't reply, and he didn't seem to take any notice of what was said to him. I went on with my work, and a few seconds afterwards, he struck me on the arm, and on the head, cutting my hat in two parts. Mutton pulled him off, and George ran down the line and laid himself across the metals. A luggage train was approaching at the time. Mutton ran towards George, and just as he was getting close, George got up and ran off in the direction of Oxenden.

Mr. Sills: Had you quarrelled with the prisoner?

Jarman: I had not really quarrelled with him. About a fortnight previously, we had a few words.

Sills: Was there not a dispute about his wife?

Jarman: I have never had a dispute with him about his wife.

Charles Henry Bland: I live at Oxenden. I am a cousin of George Bland. On the morning of the 20th of April, I met him at the George Inn at Oxenden, and we had something to drink together. I asked him what was the matter, and he said: "I have done it, Harry, and it's all through Sam", meaning Samuel Jarman. I noticed blood on one of his hands, and also on his trousers. He said: "I am off to drown myself." I saw him trying to wipe the blood off his hand. Shortly afterwards, he went off in the direction of Market Harborough. He was going there to pay his club.

Joseph Collier: I am a police sergeant in the Leicestershire County Constabulary. I apprehended the prisoner on the evening of the 20th of April, at Tur Langton, about eleven or twelve miles from his house.

I met him in the street, carrying a pail of milk. I tapped him on the shoulder and asked him his name. He replied that his name was Chester. I told him that I should apprehend him on suspicion of being George James Bland who was wanted for the murder of his wife that morning. I cautioned him, and he then said: "I am innocent. You have got the wrong man." I noticed blood on the trousers he was wearing. On going along the street, he ground his teeth, and looked up to the sky, and then said: "Temporary insanity", and he repeated that three times. He said: "Yes, that will be it." I also noticed blood in his finger nails, and on the way to the station house, he asked to be allowed to wash his hands. He said the blood came from a scratch on his hand. I took him to Little Bowden. On the way, he said: "Sergeant, man to man, God to witness, are you going to betray me?" On searching him, I found a letter from his wife.

Ellen Miller: I am the wife of Benjamin Miller, living at Hulcote, near Towcester. I am the mother of the dead woman. My daughter came to my house on the 6th of April, and remained till the 13th of April. She received a letter from Bland while she was at my house, which she left behind. [Two letters were produced, and read out by Mr. Jacques, assisting Sills for the prosecution. They showed good terms existing between the couple. His letter was despondent, on account of his being unsuccessful in finding work]

Jacques: Did the two live happily together?

Ellen Miller: Not always.

Mr. Lloyd, cross examining for the defence): Was the prisoner depressed when he was at your house in the previous March?

Ellen Miller: I cannot say he was.

Lloyd: Is it not true that a man had to remain with him all night, to prevent him from killing himself?

Ellen Miller: A man named Wilford had to remain with him, but I did not know that it was to prevent him killing himself.

Lloyd: Did the prisoner go to a pond, one morning, and say what a nice place it was?

Ellen Miller: I do not remember that.

Judge: Mrs. Miller, if a man named Wilford had to stay with your son in law, what was the reason?

Ellen Miller: It was to prevent him killing himself.

Superintendent Botterill gave evidence of charging Bland; and the surgeon, James Craig, gave pathological evidence as in the inquest.

Louisa Wallace: I am the wife of Inspector Wallace, of the Northamptonshire County Constabulary. On Wednesday the 25th of April, I saw the prisoner in his cell, when I was passing. He said: "Oh, Missus, what shall I do? I can't think whatever made me do it. I am sorry I done it, but she's an angel in Heaven now. I never thought I should come to this."

Isaac Ward, a prosecution witness, was called by Mr. Sills to give evidence of seeing Bland leaving the scene of the murder.

He was then cross examined by Mr. Lloyd.

Lloyd: When you saw the prisoner early on the 20th of April, what was he doing?

Ward: He was walking from Naseby to Kelmarsh. He was walking at the rate of about five miles an hour, and was swinging his arms in an unusual manner, almost over his head. He said "Good Morning" as he passed me.

The last prosecution witness, Edward Thomas Wheeler, described Bland removing dried blood from his arms, at the George Inn at Oxenden.

Mr. Lloyd, addressing the jury: There is no dispute that the prisoner took the life of his wife, but the question for you, the jury, is whether he was in a condition to be responsible for his actions. When we look at the facts of the case, and the supplementary evidence which I shall call before you, I think you will have no doubt that when he took his wife's life, he was not conscious of the act he was performing, and was not responsible for that act. I ask you to recall the open way in which Bland acted after the event. There is also a series of facts that prove that he was not responsible for his actions, but was really of unsound mind. I ask you to say in your judgment, that, at the time he committed the act, he was not master of his understanding. If you find this as your verdict, he would not be then set free, but would be confined during Her Majesty's Pleasure. I shall call further witnesses, now, to prove that, on his mother's side, insanity has prevailed in the family, and also that the prisoner's great uncle has been confined in an asylum.

Several witnesses, called by Lloyd testified along those lines.

Baron Huddleston summed up, and at 4 p.m. the jury retired. The verdict came at 4.25 p.m.: "Not Guilty on the Ground of Insanity." George Bland had taken little notice throughout proceedings, and now that he was to be sentenced, seemed blank.

Judge: George James Bland, you will be detained during Her Majesty's Pleasure.

THE LAST MAN TO HANG (1914)

The Soke and City of Peterborough were part of Northamptonshire until 1974. When John Francis Eayres. a tinsmith, murdered hiswife in Peterborough, in 1914, his trial took place in Northampton, and he suffered capital punishment there. The reader will surely know of Alfred Arthur Rouse, sentenced to death in Northampton, for the notorious "blazing car" murder in 1930. By then, there was no prison in Northampton, and Rouse was executed at Bedford.

The Peterborough murder took place during the first month of war, in 1914. The background to the events of 22nd August is best described by those who knew John and Sarah Eayres. Several friends and neighbours gave evidence at the trial. John Francis Eayres, aged 59, was before Sir Horace Edmund Avory (later to earn a reputation as a "hanging judge") at Northampton Assizes on Wednesday, 21st October 1914. He had been indicted for the murder of Sarah Ann Eayres. When the charge was read, and he was asked to plead, he said: "I don't know anything about it at all. I am not guilty".

The first witness was Thomas Hawksworth, of Hill's Yard, behind Bridge Street. He had seen John Eayres twice on the morning of 22nd August. On the second occasion, as they were talking, Mrs. Eayres came along the street, and John complained about her drinking habits. He gave her some money, which she took into a nearby draper's shop.

Bernard Campion,(defending Eayres): How often have you met and talked to the prisoner during your acquaintance?

Hawksworth: Practically every day.

Campion: What sort of person is he?

Hawksworth: He is quiet. A well disposed man.

Campion: Did you know that he had consulted a doctor about headaches.

Hawksworth: I did not know that.

Mrs. Elizabeth Griffin, the wife of a gardener, had lived opposite the couple for two years, at School Place, Albert Place. She knew that they had not lived happily because of Mrs. Eayres' drinking. About six o'clock on 22nd August, she saw Sarah Eayres come out of their house. She was crying, and John was running after her. Sarah shouted: "Give me my money and I'll do the shopping." John said: "I'll give you shopping, you bitch. I'll do you in before the night is out." They both went up the passage leading into their house. Half an hour later, Mrs. Griffin saw Eayres talking in the street to another neighbour, Harry Carter. Mrs. Eayres was at an upstairs window, "making faces".

Harry Carter himself gave evidence. While he and Eayres were talking, Sarah, at the upper window, shouted down to them: "Don't believe what the old liar says". Eayres shouted back: "Get down or I'll black your face". Harry Carter had frequently heard them quarrelling, and had often seen Sarah the worse for drink.

Another School Place resident, Harry George Masters, a machine operative, had also heard much quarrelling. Sarah had often been under the influence of alcohol, but John Eayres never. On that August evening, he saw them struggling on the pavement in School Place. Sarah was on the ground, and John on top of her. Masters had gone out to part them, but before he reached them, Sarah wriggled free and ran into Albert Place. Eayres went into the house. A few minutes later, Eayres reappeared and went in the direction his wife had gone; but evidently he did not find her, because Sarah returned to their home alone.

John Eayres came back, and it was at this point that Sarah began her performance at the bedroom window. Masters said that John shouted up to her: "You old bitch. You'll get what you are asking for, before morning". Sarah had locked the doors, but John put his shoulder to one and forced it open. He went inside briefly, but then emerged and went into their back yard. Masters heard glass breaking. Suddenly Sarah ran out of the side door, and she too went into the back yard. Masters surprisingly testified that they both seemed sober.

The Eayres' next door neighbour, William Rogers, of 13 Albert Place, was the next witness. He had heard the prisoner's threat to his wife that he would "do her in". At twenty minutes to ten on the night of 22nd August, he heard moaning in the Eayres' back yard, and went to investigate. He found John Lying beneath the livingroom window. He had no coat on, and there was a wound on his throat which was bleeding over his shirt. "What's happened?" asked Rogers, but John Eayres did not reply. The neighbour went into Bridge Street and found a policeman, P.C. Powley. When they returned, a few minutes later, they found the dead body of Sarah Eayres lying in the yard.

P.C. Powley gave the details in his evidence: "Eayres was semiconscious. He had a wound two inches long, on the left side of the throat, and was taken to the Infirmary. At the bottom of the yard, was the body of Mrs. Eayres, lying face downwards, fully dressed, with a pool of blood each side of her. Her hands were folded under her. There was a large gash on the right side of her face. In the scullery, I found blood in the sink, and on the floor, and on a tub. There was a bloodstained razor, closed, on the window ledge. The spot where I found Eayres was ten yards from where the woman was lying. I looked to see if there was any blood on the ground between them, but there was none. The putty had been removed from one of the panes of the livingroom window, but the glass had not been taken out. In the livingroom a glass sugar basin had been broken. There was a poker lying on the table, and at the foot of the stairs, I found a hatchet. There were a few spots of blood inside the house. A bloodstained jacket and vest were on a side table in the living room".

Dr. R. Jolley: I am Police Surgeon at Peterborough. I examined the deceased woman, Sarah Ann Eayres. The wound in her neck was a very large one. It commenced under the left ear, and extended down to the left side of the breast bone. It was an inch deep in the upper part, and gradually became shallower. All the arteries and veins on that side of the neck had been severed, and her jacket and dress had been cut through. There were cuts on the back of the first two fingers of the left hand, and there was a wound on the inside of the second finger of the same hand. I also examined the prisoner, John Francis Eayres. He had a slight superficial wound in the left side of the neck, which might have been caused by a pocketknife.

Bernard Campion (cross examining): As a medical practitioner, you have treated the prisoner as a patient, earlier this year, have you not?

Dr. Jolley: That is true. He was complaining of giddiness.

Campion: Is it true that relatives of the prisoner have been confined in asylums?

Dr. Jolley: That is not within my knowledge.

That concluded the prosecution case. Eayres elected to give evidence on his own behalf.

John Eayres: I went home for the last time, at eight o'clock on the night of the 22nd of August. Earlier, I had quarrelled with my wife. It was the same quarrel we had the previous night, all over a halfpenny.

Counsel for the Prosecution: What did your wife say to you?

Eayres, looking round the Court: There are ladies present. Must I say?

Counsel: Yes.

Eayres: She used bad language. She called me a liar. In the house, she picked up a knife and threatened me. I took the knife away, and then she threw a glass sugar basin at me. It hit me in the eye, and I have no knowledge of anything that happened after that. After throwing the basin at me, she left the house, and I didn't see her again. I didn't recollect any more until I found myself in the Infirmary, two days later. The police wouldn't tell me why I was there.

Bernard Campion, addressing the jury, submitted that a verdict of manslaughter was the most that was justified by the evidence. The prisoner's life, he said, had been made miserable by his wife. The threats that he was said to have uttered were merely exaggerated expressions that did not represent any real intention. The killing was an act committed on the impulse of a moment, after great provocation, and was free of malice. To be murder, there must be malice aforethought.

Judge Avory, summing up, told the jury that there was no ground for suggesting that the prisoner was not responsible for his actions, or that he was insane. A blow might have been sufficient provocation to reduce the offence to manslaughter, but that could only be in a case where the killer, smarting under the indignity of the blow, immediately turned upon his assailant, and either with a weapon in his hands at the time, or with one lying close by, inflicted a blow in the heat of the moment, which resulted in death. But if the killer sought for a weapon, said the Judge, the case would be one, not of manslaughter, but of murder.

The verdict came after ten minutes: "Wilful Murder".

Eayres was asked if he had anything to say. "Nothing".

The Judge assumed the black cap, and passed sentence. "John Francis Eayres, the jury have returned the only verdict which honest men, doing their duty, could return in this case. It is my painful duty to pass upon you the sentence which the law has decreed for the crime you have committed, and the sentence is that you be taken hence to a lawful prison, and then to a place of execution, and that you be there hanged by the neck until you be dead, and that your body be afterwards buried within the precincts of the prison wherein you shall have been last confined prior to your execution. And may the Lord have mercy upon your soul".

John Eayres heard it unmoved.

At Northampton Gaol, shortly before eight o'clock on the morning of Monday, 9th November 1914, Eayres, between two warders, in the middle of a little procession, reached the doors of the execution shed. He was wearing a drab prison suit. His cotton shirt, collarless, was open at the neck. His hands were pinioned behind his back. A large screen had been put up to hide the entrance of the shed from any would be observers. As they approached the warder standing at the entrance, Eayres gave a small nod and said, very quietly, "Good morning". Three more steps, and he would be inside, and in full view of the gallows. He stopped, and half turned to the same warder, and in a low voice, heard distinctly by all those present, said: "I am going to die for a bad woman, you know". The Executioner. forty year old John Ellis, from Rochdale, stood inside the shed, looking at the watch in his hand. As the procession entered, his assistant, William Willis, fell in at the rear and walked behind.

The voice of the Prison Chaplain, the Reverend J. Evan Hopkins, was now heard reciting the Service for the Burial of the Dead.

John Eayres stepped forward on to the marked trapdoor over the drop. Ellis deftly pulled the white cap down over his head and fastened it under the chin. At the same time, Willis was strapping his legs. Then Ellis fixed the noose around his neck. As soon as this was done, Ellis, with another rapid movement, stepped to the corner and pulled the lever. The drop was five feet. Only seconds after Eayres had entered the shed, only his white shrouded head, hanging listlessly to one side, was visible above the open pit. The clock of the nearby Church of the Holy Sepulchre, "Saint Sepulchre's", was still striking eight.

THE SHARP END OF A SHOEMAKER'S FILE (1901)

Aleck and Louisa Claydon lived unhappily together opposite the side wall of the Northampton Workhouse, at Number 7 Portland Street, in a row of artisans' houses. The street, which linked the Wellingborough Road with the Kettering Road, has disappeared. The Workhouse is now St. Edmund's Hospital, and its wall still stands.

After ten miserable years of marriage, the Claydons had separated by court order in 1899. Aleck had been back to court several times for failing to keep up with maintenance payments, and had been imprisoned briefly for that; but at Christmas 1900, there was a reconciliation. He returned to Portland Street to live with Louisa, young Aleck, aged ten, and Kate Wareing, Louisa's 18 year old daughter of her first marriage.

Many of the Northampton shoemakers had steady employment in the modern factories that had opened since 1889, but some, like Aleck, preferred the old system of working independently at home. He had a workshop at the back of the house, and drew out the leather from a factory, to make up into boots. The old style shoemen, lacking factory discipline, occasionally lost the urge to work. In 1901, the South African War kept the Northampton shoe trade busy, but Aleck Claydon was not working.

During the first week of July, the Claydons were seriously short of funds. Aleck had drunk away his spare cash. Louisa earned a small amount by doing washing, but it did not pay the rent, and the boy Aleck's savings had been drawn out of his Post Office Savings Bank account for that purpose.

On 6th July 1901, Aleck spent Saturday evening in a beer shop. He was unable to buy his own drinks, but he had an earthy, ungrammatical wit, and a pleasing appearance (short, thickset figure, drooping moustache) so his friends would usually treat him. When he returned home, before midnight, Louisa went straight to bed, probably to show her displeasure. At about two o'clock on Sunday morning, Aleck stunned her with a blow on the side of her head with his shoemaker's file. He thrust a corner of the bedquilt down her throat to stifle her cries, and then stabbed her repeatedly in the face with the sharp end of the file, finally burying it up to the handle in her left breast. To be sure she was dead, he took a shoemaker's awl and stabbed her in the side of her neck. He then went downstairs and ate some bread and butter. He returned to the bedroom, climbed into bed with his dead wife, and went to sleep. When he awoke, he placed a pillow over Louisa's head, and left the house. Eventually he gave himself up to P.C. Bailey at Moulton police house.

At 10 a.m. the murder was discovered by Kate, Claydon's stepdaughter. She was too scared to enter the blood spattered room, and went to fetch the landlady of "The Engineer", a public house at the corner of the street. A cyclist was sent to the Central Police Station. Chief Inspector Bates and Sub Inspector Allen took a cab and drove to Portland Street. A number of constables were already gathered in the street, which was visited by thousands of sightseers during that Sunday. Sergeant MacLeod went on his bicycle to the Borough Police Station, and made telephone calls to all the stations in the area, not knowing that, at the time, Claydon was already in custody, and on his way in a cab to the Borough Station. The two inspectors examined the bedroom at 7 Portland Street. By the bedside was the file, covered with blood and hair. Louisa's body was removed to the mortuary.

The inquest was opened on Monday morning by the Northampton Borough Coroner, C. C. Becke, but after Kate Wareing's evidence of identification, and P.C. Bailey's evidence of arrest, it was adjourned to the following Monday.

Aleck Claydon was taken before the Mayor, F. G. Adnitt; and five other magistrates at the Guildhall at 10.30 a.m. He wore a grey suit and waistcoat, with a yellow pansy in the buttonhole. He smiled faintly at the Clerk when answering the formal questions. The charge was read to him: "that you did feloniously kill and murder one Louisa Claydon, your wife, in a bedroom at 7 Portland Street at some time between 11 p.m. on Saturday 6th July 1901 and 9.45 a.m. on Sunday, July 7th, 1901..." Police evidence of the crime, and of Claydon's arrest, was given. Claydon was asked if he wished to question the officers. After Bailey's evidence, he said: "There is nothing I wish to ask him, only he met me yesterday when I was lost." The Clerk said: "I think you had better say nothing now." Claydon: "Perhaps it would be as well." He was remanded for one week.

During that week, the Chief Constable applied to the Treasury for legal assistance with the prosecution. Reporters from many newspapers interviewed those who were connected with the case. Some who had seen the corpse described it as "the most horrible spectacle they had ever seen". Some gave accounts entirely different from the versions they would later give in Court. Policemen told them that Aleck Claydon was eating heartily, and seemed "as happy as a bird".

Committal proceedings took place in the Guildhall at 10.30 a.m. on Monday 15th July. Alderman Cleaver deputised for the Mayor who had to be at his parlour all day, receiving donations for the memorial to the late Queen Victoria. A. J. Darnell, appointed by the Treasury to prosecute, announced that the case would be heard de novo (a fresh start).

Kate Wareing, Aleck Claydon's stepdaughter, in deep mourning, was allowed to give her evidence seated. She testified that Claydon had arrived home at 11.15 on that Saturday night, slightly drunk. "Mother went to bed instantly, and so did I. Around two o'clock, my lamp was lit in my bedroom. I shouted for Ma. I asked what he wanted it lit for. He said he wanted something to eat. I told him to blow it out and go to bed; and he did so, latching both bedroom doors. I heard nothing and knew nothing, till just before ten on Sunday morning. I went to Mother's room to call her for breakfast. Everything was covered with blood, and I went to get help. He had been on the drink for a fortnight. Mother and him had words about it. She said she couldn't live with him any longer because he refused to get work.

Claydon: What my daughter stated, she has said the truth, but then as regards the work, I couldn't get work.

He was interrupted by the Assistant Clerk who warned him not to make a statement.

Susan Langley: I am the landlady of "The Engineer" publichouse. When I was called in, I found the deceased lying on the bed in a pool of blood, quite dead. There was a tassel [produced] off the edge of a quilt, in her mouth. I tried to lift her head up, but it was stuck to the pillow by blood, and the pillow came up as well. There was a file on the bed.

A shoemaker's file was produced, fourteen inches long, one inch wide. At one end was a sharp spike, two inches long, all covered with blood and hair. P. C. Herbert Wooding told how he had taken possession of it, when he had arrived at the scene of the murder. He had sent for the Police Surgeon, and remained with the body until it was removed to the mortuary.

Isaac Finedon: I am the landlord of the "Old Globe" beerhouse, on the Kettering Road. On Saturday night, Aleck Claydon came in, but he had no money, and I refused to serve him. He remained for about two hours, and had drinks with his friends. He went out once, but returned. About nine Mrs. Claydon came in with washing, and I gave her a glass of ale. Claydon went and whispered in her ear, but she turned away and gave no answer. She left then. [Claydon in the dock, smiled broadly] Claydon left at eleven. He was perfectly sober.

Aleck Claydon was asked if he had any questions for that witness, and said: "Why, Mr. Finedon, your statement's wrong from beginning to end."

Joseph Lack: I am a labourer. I live at Kingsthorpe. At nine o'clock on Sunday morning, I saw Aleck Claydon at "The Telegraph" public house at Moulton, and we got into a conversation over a black dog I had with me. We sat on a bench together, outside. He said: "I feel 'dicky'. I've been on the booze this last fortnight." He said: "I've got something to tell you – a story. I went out last night and had a pint or two of beer. I left my wife in the bar and went into the parlour, and stayed until closing time, and went home. My wife was abed, asleep. I got into bed with her, and she said she should sooner have a serpent beside her than me. I laid down and went to sleep. Then I went down to my workshop and fetched my rasp. I hit her on the forehead, and stabbed her in the heart." I said: "You're romancing. You must have got the blues, talking such rubbish." He then says: "I'm got a knife in my pocket. I shall have to do for myself." I says: "Don't talk like that. Put it away." We went out together. When we got to the Old Bluebell Inn, he said: "That's the old place I've used many a time. I should like to go in there for the last time. You buy a pint, and I'll go to the police with you." We went to P.C. Bailey's house at Moulton, and called him up. Claydon gave himself up.

Aleck Claydon: I never asked you to go to no constable. I've knowed where he lives for the last twenty eight years.

P.C. Bailey, Northamptonshire County Police: I met the prisoner at 5.45 a.m. on a side road near Buttock's Booth. He enquired the way to Moulton, but he went away in the direction of Boughton. At 9.45, he came with Lack to my station. He said: "I didn't think you were stationed here, when I met you this morning. Did you think I was in a mizzy mozzy? I believe I have murdered my wife." I cautioned him. He then unbuttoned his coat and showed me some bloodstains on the front of his shirt, and on the palms of his hands. He said: "That tells a tale." He made a statement [Bailey read from it]: "...Last night at 9.15, I met my wife in the Old Globe, on the Kettering Road. I asked if she was all right. She said: 'Are you?' and I said, 'Yes'. I remained there till eleven, and then went home directly, and up to bed. I had no light. My wife was in bed. She called me a dirty dog, and said she would sooner have a serpent to sleep with her than me. I said nothing, and did nothing. I then went to sleep until one a.m. I believe I got up and went down to my shop and got my file; and I struck her on the head with it. I then went downstairs and had two eggs and some bread and butter... I went back to bed and slept till a quarter to four. When I woke, I put my hand on my wife's body, and found it was cold. I then got up and went for a walk."

Claydon: I think that my statement ought not to have been taken in the state I was by no policeman or any officer.

Sub Inspector Allen: ...Going upstairs into the front bedroom, I saw the deceased on a bed, which stood just in front of the door. She was lying on her right side, dead. The bedclothes were all saturated with blood, and the wall beside her was besmeared with blood. I lifted her up and examined her. On the left side of her head, near the temple, was a large scalp wound, two inches long and very deep. On the left side of the neck was a hole, apparently from a stab, two inches below the left ear; and another just under the left breast, and over the heart, all of which appeared to have been done by the end of the file [produced] which had blood, flesh and hair on it. The left arm, which was raised from the body in an attitude of defence, was covered with bruises, extending from the wrist to the shoulder, and there were several stabs near the elbow, the bone of which appeared to be broken. Her fingers were clenched, and between them I found several short hairs which corresponded with the hair on the prisoner's head. I took possession of them. [produced] There did not appear to have been a struggle, as the bedclothes were in order, and the furniture was not disarranged. The hair on the file corresponded with that on the head of the deceased... I charged Aleck Claydon with wilful murder. He replied: "Well, I see. I left home at 3.45 a.m., and one of your officers saw me. It was striking four o'clock when I passed the bottom of Palmerston Road. I woke up at one o'clock. I think the job was done, then..." I conveyed him to the Central Police Station in a cab... He was taken to the cells, and his shirt taken from him. [produced, showing large blood spots on the front] He and his wife had a judicial separation on January 4th 1899. I know that the prisoner and the deceased came together again soon after Christmas, and have been living together since.

That concluded the evidence against Aleck Claydon, and when asked, he said: "I have nothing to say." He was committed to take his trial at the November Assizes. The proceedings had taken two hours.

At 3.15 on the afternoon of that same Monday, the adjourned inquest was resumed in the Sessions Court of the Guildhall. Claydon was present, in custody. The same witnesses gave the same evidence. Medical evidence had not been called by the magistrates, a possible reason for the detailed description given by Inspector Allen; but pathological testimony was necessary at the inquest. Dr. Cropley said that the penetration of the heart, between the third and fourth ribs, was done after death had already occurred. The cause of death was probably massive loss of blood. The file was confirmed as the likely cause of the wounds.

The inquest jury found a verdict of "Wilful Murder". They gave their fees to the young son of the deceased, to replace the money he had drawn from his Post Office savings.

C. C. Becke, Coroner: That is very good of you. The boy will have one pound, six shillings, and it shall be placed to his credit in the bank. Stand up, Claydon. I now commit you to take your trial at the ensuing Assizes. Do you want to say anything?

Aleck Claydon: No, sir. I've already said enough.

Coroner: I should think so. How old was your wife?

Claydon: Fortythree.

Coroner to Chief Inspector Bates: You can now remove the prisoner under my warrant as well as that of the Borough Magistrates.

On Thursday, 23rd November, 1901, the second day of the Northampton Assizes, Aleck Claydon, in the same grey suit, with a white knotted tie and a "standup" collar, stood before the Honourable Sir John Charles Bigham. The Court was packed, with many standing, and hundreds outside. The previous afternoon, the Grand Jury had returned a True Bill against him (confirmed that there was a case to answer). His manner was no longer nonchalant, and there were new lines on his forehead. He was undefended, but the Judge appointed Ryland Adkins to conduct his defence.

Lacey Smith, opening the prosecution, on behalf of the Treasury, suggested that there was much evidence of premeditation. "The prisoner said to a boon companion, just before: 'Would you be surprised if I done a murder?'"

Adkins argued that Claydon came from a family "drenched with insanity, and burdened with a curse only one little bit less dreadful that of drink. Bred of lunatics and tainted with drink, at the time of the murder, he was not earning money, and was giving his time to self indulgence... Can you imagine the man sleeping with the woman after he had murdered her? The violence he used was wholly unnecessary where one blow was sufficient to cause death."

Judge Bigham, summing up: ...There is not the ghost of evidence that there was anything of the nature of a quarrel, and the prisoner has not even suggested it. When a man deliberately goes away to fetch an instrument with which he then kills his wife, that is NOT manslaughter. This is a case of murder, and the only real question is whether, when he did the act, he knew that he was doing wrong. The fact that he was drunk is no excuse for crime. I need not tell you of the consequences which might follow from your verdict. That is nothing to do with you.

The verdict was "Guilty".

Clerk of the Assizes: Prisoner at the Bar, your arraignment charges you with wilful murder, and upon that you put yourself on your country. Your country has found you guilty. Have you anything to say why the Court should not proceed to pass sentence upon you, and why you should not die, according to law?

The Judge's Marshal placed the black cap upon the head of the Judge, saying: "My Lord, the King's justice strictly commands that all persons are to keep silent whilst the sentence of death is pronounced." Claydon was supported by the Chief Warder and his assistants.

Judge: Aleck Claydon, you have been found guilty, on evidence which I think to be irresistible, of the murder of your wife. It was a cruel, heartless murder. I may say this: that I daresay it would not have happened if you had not given way to this horrible vice of drunkenness, but the fact that you gave way to that vice, and that has undoubtedly led you to commit the crime, affords, in my eyes, no extenuation. It remains the same wicked and cruel murder. I shall say no more except this: that I advise you to prepare yourself for the end, which I believe is very near. The sentence upon you is that you be taken hence to the place of execution, and that you be there hanged by the neck until you be dead, and that your body be buried within the precincts of the prison in which you were last confined. And may the Lord have mercy upon your soul.

Many voices said: "Amen".

Aleck Clayton was hanged at 8 a.m., on Friday 13th December 1901, by the brothers Billington, and his body was placed under an "initialled slab" in the yard of the Northampton Borough Gaol.

Billington senior, who had hanged the three previous murderers capitally convicted at Northampton, MacRae, Sabey and Parker, was too ill to do this job, and delegated the duty to his sons. They returned home to Bolton, to find him dead.

A LYNCHING (1322)

On a day in March 1322, Henry Felip and his son were heading home to Stoke Bruerne from Northampton. At Courteenhall they were waylaid by six robbers. Felip quickly thrust his coins into his son's hand. "Take the money. Go and get help." He turned to face the robbers, and his son ran round them out of their reach. At nearby Courteenhall young Felip raised the hue and cry. It was the law that all who heard a cry of alarm, when a crime was committed or discovered, were bound to give assistance, without delay. It was the medieval equivalent of dialling 999.

Followed by willing Courteenhall men, young Felip ran back to the scene of the incident. Too late! His father lay dead on the ground. The griefstricken young man had to decide, quickly, whether to stay with his father's corpse, or go with the others in an attempt to catch up with the killers, identify them and apprehend them. In the distance, figures could be seen running towards Northampton. His father's murderers had to be caught.

After a chase, five of the six miscreants were overtaken and arrested.

The sixth, turned off the road to the right, heading towards the church of Wootton. When Felip and some of his helpers arrived, the robber was inside and safe from capture.

The law of sanctuary gave full protection to any fugitive, however serious the crime he or she had committed, so long as certain procedures were properly carried out. The punishment for violating sanctuary was severe, so Felip and his companions could do no more than stand helplessly at the door. Only a few days before this, two soldiers from Cold Ashby had killed the man who had recruited them by shoving a lance through his body.

They had then gone into Cold Ashby Church and claimed sanctuary, thus escaping punishment for their crime.

The next step for the robber in Wootton Church was to confess his guilt to the Coroner. Richard Luvell, of Farthingstone, Coroner, was duly sent for, and arrived on Wednesday 24th March, with witnesses from Wootton and the three nearest villages.

The fugitive gave his name, John of Ditchford. He confessed that he had participated in the murder of Henry Felip at Courteenhall.

70

"Do you abjure the realm?" asked the Coroner.

"What does that mean?"

"You have to agree to leave the country and never return. If you come back you can be executed for your crime."

The alternative was a hanging, so John of Ditchford abjured the realm. The port of Dover was assigned to him. He was required to give up all his possessions. A sword, a knife and clothing were taken from him, valued at 18 pence. He was given sackcloth to wear, and a small wooden cross to hold. He was told to walk directly to Dover. If he left the King's highway, he could be arrested. At Dover he would stand kneedeep in the sea until the next ship was leaving. He had to be on it. If he carried out all those instructions, he was safe from punishment for his confessed crime of murder.

All this must have been frustrating for Henry Felip's son, and those who sympathised with him. Robbery with violence, on the roads around Northampton, was not a rare occurrence. The five robbers who had been captured would surely be hanged. It seemed a pity that this one should get away with it.

Clutching his little cross, John of Ditchford set off southwards, wearing his sackcloth robe. Two days later, he was found dead, minus his head, in the fields of Collingtree.

He had travelled less than a mile.

Richard Luvell, Coroner, now had a different task. He presided over an inquest into the cause of death of John of Ditchford.

The jurymen came from Wootton, Collingtree, Courteenhall and Rothersthorpe. They heard evidence that the deceased man had set off along the highway, heading for the assigned seaport of Dover. Near Collingtree, he suddenly left the King's highway and ran towards the woods. Spectators following at a distance had raised the hue and cry, so there was a chase. His head was cut off while he was trying to escape. He was in breach of sanctuary. No evidence was heard that Henry Felip's son had been involved.

The Coroner ordered the jurymen to carry the dead man's head to the King's Castle at Northampton.

Exactly ten years later, the Sheriff ordered an election for a new Coroner to replace Richard Luvell, because his qualifications were insufficient.

ILLUSTRATIONS

1. *Cold Higham: probable site of Mayne's Well and 1329 murder.*

2. *Holcot: cottage row opposite pond. Scene of 1871 murder.*

3. *The former "King of Denmark", St. Edmund's Road, Northampton.*

4. *Thorpelands: scene of the ambush and assassination of Speaker Tresham, 1450.*

5. & 6. *The Militia Stores, later Territorial Army HQ, Clare Street, Northampton. (Scene of 1878 murders).*

7. *Corby: ventilation shaft above railway tunnel. (Number Seven Shaft in 1879.*

8. & 9. *Portland Place, Northampton: site of 7 Portland Street, scene of 1901 murder.*

10. *Rushden: land between the Bedford Road (A6), scene of 1891 murder.*

11. *Chaucer Street, Kingsley Park, Northampton: scene of 1904 murder.*

12. *The main line at Harlestone. Jack Ray's victim was found here in 1985.*

13. *Northampton Sessions House (venue for murder trials). The County Gaol was behind it.*

14. *The final resting place of executed murderers from the Northampton Borough Gaol. When it closed, their bodies were re-interred here in the Towcester Road Cemetery.*

1.

2.

3.

4.

5.

6.

7.

8.

9.

10.

11.

12

13

14.

A RUSHDEN MYSTERY (1891)

It seems an alarming statement to say that several murderers who committed their crimes in and around Rushden, were never caught. An example is the unexplained shooting of three travellers in their caravan parked in Ditchford Lane in 1981. Ninety years before that, the town was alive with rumours as to the identity of the killer of Joe Dickens.

At the age of 72, Joseph Dickens was still in regular employment as a farm labourer. In 1891 there was no old age pension, and the rent had to be paid to his Wellingborough landlord for his cottage at the extreme south end of Rushden. Joe was unmarried, but since the death of his housekeeper in 1889, George and Fanny Jackson had moved in with him.

On Wednesday, 21st January 1891, Joe was at his cottage for his midday meal, provided by Mrs. Jackson. At 1.50 p.m., with his pipe in his mouth, he set off to do a job of hedgecutting. At dusk, he failed to arrive at Wylde's Farm for milking. A search party went out to look for him, but in the darkness, in rough, uneven terrain, as it still is, he was not found.

The search was resumed the next morning, and the body was found by two men, Childs and Tomlinson, at 7.55 a.m., at a point where two fields were linked by a footbridge. Joe Dickens was lying on his back in a pool of bloodreddened water. Police Sergeant Oram took charge. Attempts had been made to conceal the body with long grass and hedge cuttings, and a trail of blood and footmarks showed that the dead man had been dragged by two persons. Nearby were bundles of grass used to wipe blood from their hands. Dickens' hat was found near where he had been working. There were gunshot wounds on his back, and his left ear had been partly severed. There was money in his pocket: twenty three shillings; so the motive was not robbery.

To find this site a century later, we travel along the Bedford Road from Rushden, past the Tecnic Shoe Factory. At the south end of the factory car park is Manor Park. The land to the east is rough ground, which, in 1891, was the farm estate, fields and hedges, where Dickens worked. His access to it was along footpaths from the Bedford Road, but it could also be entered from the adjoining Higham Park Farm on the east. Game rights over Wylde's Farm belonged to Herbert Sartoris of Rushden Hall, and he employed a Rushden shoerivetter, Thomas Childs (the finder of the body) as part-time gamekeeper.

The inquest opened at 2 p.m. on Saturday, 24th January, in the Vestry Hall. The police investigation was still proceeding, now under the directions of a Superintendent and an Inspector from Wellingborough; and Rushden was buzzing with rumours about poachers, and about individuals who may have had grudges against the old man. The jury was sworn: every member a prominent Rushden resident. The Coroner, J. T. Parker, addressed them: "...The deceased was a man you have all doubtless known as an inoffensive, respectable citizen; and if there is one thing more clear than another, it is that he has come by his death through brutal violence. It appears that he went to his work on the afternoon of Wednesday the 21st, and as he did not come home again, a search was made for him, but he could not be found that night. The next morning, however, his body was found in a ditch, with a wound on the head, and he appeared to have been shot through the back whilst lying down, and by a gun that was placed close to his body. If that is so, it is clearly a case of murder, and it is your duty to enquire if it is so; and if you can, to say who was guilty of the crime. The evidence is not conclusive against anybody... We shall go as far as we can, today, and if the police think it necessary, we can adjourn in order to give an opportunity for bringing further evidence. If you do not wish to be called together again, it rests with you to say that murder has been committed by some persons unknown. Such a verdict would allow the police to go on with the case, and if a culprit is found, they can bring him before Magistrates. An adjournment might indeed be useful, as I have power to compel witnesses to attend and give evidence. The police have not... I hope every citizen in the place will turn himself into an amateur detective... It is, if not a disgrace, a slur upon a place of this size, that a murder should be committed and the murderer go undiscovered..."

The jury then left to view the body. They had to walk to the Dickens' cottage at the very edge of the town. He was laid out on the floor. On their return to the Vestry Hall, they began to hear the witnesses.

Fanny Jackson: I am the wife of George Jackson. The deceased is Joseph Dickens. He was a farm labourer, and occupied a bit of land. He was 72 years of age. My husband and I live in the same house he lived in. On Wednesday, he came home to his dinner as usual, about twenty minutes past one; and he left the house again shortly before two o'clock to go back to work. He usually returned about halfpast five, but he didn't do so on Wednesday. I made enquiries, and told his employer, Mr. Wylde. I never saw Joe again till he was brought home dead.

George Skinner, a juror, asked if he had seemed normal.

Fanny: He seemed to enjoy his dinner, and he lit his pipe afterwards.

Skinner: Did you know he was carrying his money with him?

Fanny: I don't know anything about that. He seldom said anything about money. I don't think he had much money, as he was a man who paid his way.

A juror: Did anybody go up the road after him when he left?

Fanny: I didn't see anyone.

Skinner: Did you know he had a bill of five pounds to make up?

Fanny: He didn't tell me that.

Skinner was a butcher, and may have been referring to money Dickens owed him for meat.

John Underwood: I am a labourer. I live in Rushden. I knew the deceased, and I saw him about a quarter to two on Wednesday afternoon, on the Bedford Road. I walked with him as far as the footpath that goes across to Higham Park. He left me there to go across the field. This path is only a hundred yards or so from the end of the village. I saw him go as far as the allotment ground, but when he got to the second field from the road, I couldn't see him no more. He went in the direction of Mr. Wylde's land, and he told me he was going back to his work. The only other person I saw was a little girl. I had to go just a short way along the road. I saw a man who was going threshing: he was going towards the town.

John Wylde: I am a farmer, at Rushden. The deceased was a labourer in my employ. On Wednesday, I sent him to trim a hedge in a field which he approached by a footpath from the Bedford Road. He started on that work about half past seven in the morning, and I saw no more of him. He ought to have come back to the farm buildings about five o'clock, but he didn't do so. In consequence of what Mrs. Jackson told me, a search was made for him, and continued all evening. We went to the field where we supposed he had been working, and while we were there, Jackson found a fork which Dickens had taken from the farm for his work that morning. The hedge trimmer was also found, close by. This was the field where Dickens had worked during the morning, but in the afternoon he had been working in another field. As far as I know he had no quarrel with his fellow workmen.

Charles Bayes, a juror: Was he a quarrelsome man?

Wylde: No he wasn't.

Foreman of the Jury, William Wilkins: Had the deceased any sum of money?

Wylde: He drew his harvest money some months ago.

A juror: Was he not robbed some time ago?

Wylde: I have lived near him for some years, and I know that his house was broken into on one occasion. I never heard him say he suspected any particular person of the robbery.

Coroner: Did the deceased tell anyone that he was carrying money about with him?

Wylde: I didn't hear him say he should carry his money about.

Coroner: Where was the exact location of his work?

Wylde: I found that during the latter part of Wednesday, he'd been cutting a hedge in a stubble field known as Lang Furlong, but the tools were found in Eight Acre Field, which is nearer to Rushden.

Thomas Tomlinson: I am a farm bailiff, living at Rushden Lodge. On Thursday morning, about a quarterpast eight, I was on the footpath leading from Higham Park to Rushden, when I met a man named

Thomas Childs coming towards me from the direction of Rushden, across the field. He had three dogs with him. He asked me if I had seen anyone up that way... I replied: "No." Childs then said: "We've lost Joe Dickens." I suggested that he should look the other side of the hedge; and I said I would look out on my way to Rushden. We went on our way, but Childs called after me, and said: "Here he is." I went back to where Childs was standing, and I saw a man's feet lying in the bottom of the ditch, which is seven or eight feet deep. I could see no more, because the body was covered over. Childs said; "Here he is. He's done it." But, I said: "He's not covered himself up!" Childs asked me to go to Mr. Wylde's farm and fetch a horse and cart, and also to tell the police. The body was not touched, and I left Childs with it, whilst I went on.

Charles Bayes, a juror: How did you know it was Dickens?

Tomlinson: I took it for granted. The body was covered up with sedge grass and hedge toppings. There was blood on the grass on the bridge close by the ditch.

Superintendent Bailie was one of the police officers on the case. He asked Tomlinson: "Did you see any sign that the body had been moved from elsewhere?"

Tomlinson: I saw marks as of the body being dragged across the stubble field, and there was blood about the field.

Thomas Childs: I am a shoe finisher, and I act sometimes as gamewatcher to Mr. Sartoris. I heard on Wednesday evening of Dickens being missed, but I didn't go in search of him that evening. I heard of it in the Compasses Inn, about seven o'clock. The next morning, I went in search, at the request of Jackson. I went up on Mr. Wylde's farm. Mr. Sartoris has the right of shooting over it. I met Mr. Tomlinson, and mentioned what I was doing. When I got about twenty five yards further on, near the occupation bridge, one of my dogs made a dart at something on the bank, and on looking in the ditch, I saw a lot of hedge trimmings there. I looked more closely, and saw a man's leg. I at once called to Mr. Tomlinson to come back. I saw some blood on the snow, and said to Mr. Tomlinson: "It looks as if he's cut his throat." I supposed it was Dickens directly I saw the body. I didn't know he'd been working there in that field. I waited with the body till the police arrived. I saw marks in the field, as if the body had been dragged about seventy yards from a hedge that had just been trimmed. I didn't see any blood on the bridge. It looked as if the body had been lifted up and dropped into the ditch. I traced a footmark as if someone had walked backwards and dragged the body towards the ditch. There was blood along the ground at intervals. The hedge trimmings appeared to have been fetched from about fifty yards, from where the body was dragged.

A juryman asked if he had seen signs of a struggle.

Childs: There were marks of a slight struggle near the hedge about seventy yards from where the body was, but I didn't see any blood there. It looked to me as if more than one man put him in the ditch, because there were many footmarks close to the body.

Jury Foreman, Wilkins: Were you out game watching on Wednesday?

Childs: I go out watching when I have no shoe work to do. I was out on Wednesday in the park, but I didn't hear the report of a gun. I didn't have my gun with me, then. I haven't taken it out during the frost, for fear of slipping down. If I'd heard a gun from that direction on Wednesday, I would've gone there. No one else has the right to carry a gun over the farm, but some do so. While I was out, I didn't see anyone up the Bedford Road with a gun.

Wilkins, Foreman: When was the last time you were in that area?

Childs: The last time I was up the fields was Sunday. I started to go up Wednesday morning, but it was too slippery and I turned back.

Several jurors closely questioned Childs about his movements on Wednesday afternoon, and about men he had seen carrying guns on the farm, but he added nothing to what he had already said.

"I was at work, shoe finishing, till half past four, Wednesday."

P.C. Arthur Haynes, stationed at Rushden: I heard on the Wednesday evening, of the deceased being missing, and I assisted others in the search. I resumed the search next morning, and about halfpast eight, I was informed by Mr. Tomlinson as to finding the body. I went to where I was directed, and saw Childs standing on the bridge near the ditch. He said: "Here lies Dickens in the dyke. He's been murdered, and covered over." On looking into the ditch, I saw a man's leg. The remainder of the body was covered over with grass and thorns. I examined the ditch, but there were no signs of anyone stepping into it. Snow was lying on both sides, and there were no marks there. On the top of the bank was blood, and footmarks. Childs pointed to a mark along the field, and it looked as though a body had been dragged along. There were footmarks both sides of where the body had been dragged. There were spots of blood on the stubble, for a distance of sixty four yards from where the body was found. Near a newly trimmed hedge, I found marks of a struggle, but no blood. I followed the same marks back to the body, and then got into the ditch. I uncovered the body, and found it to be Dickens. He was fully dressed, but no hat; lying on his back, with his right leg over the left. I searched his clothes and found twenty five shillings in a bag in the lefthand trousers pocket. There was also a knife and some tobacco. I had some assistance in lifting the body on to the bank, and I saw a wound on the head. The clothes on his back, under the right shoulder, were saturated with blood, and there was a hole in his throat. He was quite dead and stiff. His clothes were not disarranged. I found his hat about eighty four yards from the body, on the other side of the hedge. About a hundred and seventy yards further on, I found a stockaxe in the hedgebottom, with bloodstains on the handle.

Charles R. Owen: I am a medical practitioner in Rushden. I saw the deceased on Thursday morning at 10.30. He had been dead some hours. He was attired in his working clothes, with hedging gloves on his hands. The clothes were wet, and his face was sprinkled with blood. I found part of the left ear severed horizontally, and the wound extended about an inch along the face, the skin then being torn in a downward direction. On the right side of his head, midway between the ear and vertex, I found a small triangular piece of flesh sticking up as though from a punctured wound on the scalp. On removing the clothes, I found a wound in the back, under the right shoulder. It appeared to be a gunshot wound, the edges being black. On Friday I made a post mortem examination of the body. I found the shot had traversed the body. Thirty two shot were found just beneath the skin of the abdomen...

P.C. Haynes produced the shot and laid them in front of the jury.

Dr. Owen: The shot had passed through one of the kidneys. I also found some undigested food in the stomach. The gunshot wound would cause death almost immediately. The wound in the back was three inches higher than where the shot was found in the abdomen. The shot must have been fired close to the body. The wound to the ear might have been occasioned by the stockaxe [also produced], the wound being very nearly the same length as its blade. The clothes where the shot entered, were singed by powder. The gunshot wound could have been inflicted whilst the deceased was either standing or lying down.

A juror made a statement which was really a question: "He was killed by the shot wounds in his kidney."

Dr. Owen: A portion of the spleen was shattered with shot, and the stomach was also riddled.

The inquest was adjourned in the expectation that further evidence would be forthcoming, but when it reopened on Saturday 7th February 1891, Superintendent Bailie attended to inform the Coroner that there was no further information.

J. T. Parker, the Coroner, addressed the jury again: "There is no reason for a further adjournment. Rewards for information lead to perjury, and should not be encouraged. If any parishioner has information which he is keeping for a reward, that is very wrong. Your verdict should be murder, not manslaughter, by persons unknown." Clearly, he believed that nothing further could be achieved, and the proceedings should be brought to an end with a verdict. The Rushden jurymen, however, were not satisfied. The Foreman, William Wilkins, asked a question: "If any gentleman wishes to have a witness here, can he do so?" "Yes," said the Coroner, "if you think any light can be thrown upon it. On the last occasion, the evidence did not point to anybody in the least. Do you wish to call any witness?"

The jury consulted in private for an hour, and then called George Jackson, whose wife, Fanny, had testified on the first day. He described the locality where the tools were found, and also his conversation with Thomas Childs, the watcher, before Joe Dickens' body was found. Finally, the verdict desired by the Coroner was brought in: "Wilful Murder by some person or persons unknown."

There were no further developments until Easter Monday, 31st March 1891. On that day, an Irthlingborough builder had business at Ditchford Station, and wandered down to the river Nene by Ditchford Mill. Peering into the water, he saw the body of a man floating upright. The body, badly decomposed, was taken out and removed to the Carpenter's Arms, at Irchester. A paysheet in a pocket, showed that he was William Attley; and that he had been working at Irchester, and pay was due to him for five and a quarter days, on February 27th.

The inquest was held on Wednesday 1st April, at the Red Lion Inn, Irchester, before J. T. Parker, the same Coroner who had presided on view of the body of Joseph Dickens. He must have remembered those proceedings, although he had officiated at several inquests since January. The jurymen were greatly distressed by the condition of Attley's body. The flesh was falling away from the limbs. Harry Attley, the brother of the deceased, said that William, known as "Whit" Attley, was a Ringstead man, aged 24, unmarried, and had lodged with him in Rushden, at 2 North Street. Harry testified that at the end of February, Whit had been acting very strangely. He "seemed queer in his mind" and was "about the place drinking for a day or two". Harry had not seen him since Thursday, 26th February, when he went to bed at ten, but left the house at 3 a.m. "They are after me with a horse and cart" were words Whit Attley had used before his disappearance, when he was acting "very strange and quiet".

Police Constable Arthur Haynes, who had been called when the body of Joseph Dickens had been found, attended the inquest on Whit Attley. He had a question for brother Harry:

"Is it true that he was under suspicion, though not by the police, for the murder of Joe Dickens?"

Harry Attley: Not as far as I know. The rumour got about after he left.

P.C. Haynes: I have been told that the accusation preyed on his mind not that he committed the murder but he knew something about it, and wouldn't tell.

The verdict was "Found drowned".

No one was ever arrested by the police on the Rushden murder case in 1891, but among Rushden townsfolk rumours were rife and accusing fingers were pointed.

At least two men were present when Joe Dickens was murdered and concealed, one of whom had a shotgun. The motive was not robbery, and no one was known to have any serious grievance against the old man. A possible reason for his murder was to silence him after he had witnessed some kind of sinister incident or activity. Joe Dickens entered that rather wild area from the main Bedford Road, but there was quieter access from the east, the Higham Park direction. January was poaching season, when evenings were dark and frosty, and cheap hot meals were wanted for the table. Suppose poachers entered that land at dusk, not realising that a man was still working in a hedge, hidden from them. Would they be ruthless enough to kill him, to prevent him identifying them to the authorities. Was the guilt stricken Whit Attley a poacher while lodging in Rushden?

Was one of them a man in a paid position of trust, armed with a shotgun?

Five years after the murder, the following legal notice was published in a local newspaper:

"APOLOGY TO MR. THOMAS CHILDS, OF BEDFORD ROAD, RUSHDEN, KEEPER.

WHEREAS I, the undersigned Charles Dickens of Bedford Road, Rushden, Labourer, have lately in a public place and in the presence of other persons made a serious statement against the above named Thomas Childs, accusing him of having been guilty of killing one Joseph Dickens, which statement I incautiously made, and for which I have no foundation whatever, and the same causing great injury to the character of the said Thomas Childs, as well as being likely to seriously affect his personal comfort and health, he has justly threatened proceedings against me, but in consideration of my agreeing to withdraw the statement I have made and apologising for same, as well as paying such a sum as is agreed towards the expenses incurred in reference to this matter, all of which I gladly do, he has consented to forbear from further proceedings against me... I hereby authorise and request the said Thomas Childs to advertise and make whatever other use of this apology he thinks fit. Dated this 18th day of May, 1896, CHARLES DICKENS X his mark.

Witness: Paul D. Ellis, Clerk to Mr. F. Newman, Solicitor, Rushden.

NOT QUITE A "SHOCKING WIFE MURDER" (1885)

In August 1885, a London publisher of sensational literature brought out a penny broadsheet bearing the heading:
"ALLEGED SHOCKING WIFE MURDER At Wellingborough"
The publisher was Henry Parker Such, steam printer, whose family brought out "gallows literature" in the form of small handbills until 1917. This one had verses intended to be sung to the tune "Teddy O'Neale".

They began as follows:
"I will say a few words on those who are drinking
That liquor that causes three parts of our crime,
And men commit murder not one moment thinking,
That death on the scaffold must reach them in time.
In Wellingborough we hear of a most cruel murder.
A woman's the victim, Mrs. Wheatley by name.
Cruelty and punishment could go no further,
And now she is dead she is free from all blame.

"Drink once again is the cause of this murder.
At Wellingborough Mrs. Wheatley lies dead,
Killed by her husband her sorrows are over,
And now she's at rest in her last lonely bed."
Further stanzas give a pious version of the circumstances of this suspicious death. Here comes the factual version.

On 28th July 1885, the news rapidly spread in Wellingborough that John Wheatley had cut his wife's throat. Several hundred sightseers congregated around their house in Hatton Park Road, and a large crowd gathered in Market Street in the expectation of seeing Wheatley taken to the Police Station.

Wheatley was 61, a native of Great Doddington, and for 17 years he had lived in Wellingborough, employed by local farmers as a shepherd. Mary, his second wife, had married him ten years earlier. A teenage boy and girl lived with them. Six other children had grown up and left home.

Mary had been seen at home alive between eleven and twelve that morning. In reply to a neighbour's enquiry about her health, she said: "I am pretty middling; much about the same." Later, the behaviour of "Shep" Wheatley convinced the neighbours that he had murdered her. He was seen handling a bloodstained knife.

On the following day, Wednesday 29th July, Wheatley was taken before a magistrate and charged by Superintendent Bailie with causing the death of his wife. He said: "I wasn't the death of her." He repeated that, and then he was removed to the cells.

The inquest was held at 6 p.m. that day, in the New Inn, Broad Green, not far from the Wheatleys' house. The jury viewed the body, and then heard the guiding words of the Divisional Coroner, J. T. Parker. "The facts of the case are few, but very painful. The question to be decided is how the deceased Mary Wheatley, who was last seen alive at 2 p.m. yesterday, came by her death. It appears that shortly after two, a neighbour was called in by Wheatley, who said: 'My wife is dead'; and the evidence, I believe, will go to prove that she did not die from natural causes, but that she was suffocated. Wheatley seems partly to admit that he did it himself, and if you are satisfied about that, it will be for you to consider whether he is guilty of murder or manslaughter. At present, I do not find that there is evidence of sufficient provocation on the part of the deceased to reduce the crime from murder to manslaughter."

The neighbours gave evidence.

Jane Spriggs: I am the wife of Samuel Spriggs, residing at 6 Hatton Park Road. On Tuesday, I was at home in my back kitchen. About half past three in the afternoon, I saw Mr. Wheatley come in the direction of my house, with only his shirt on, and with blood on his face. On seeing me, he said: "I have done..." I did not catch the next word. "My wife is dead." I said: "No, Mr. Wheatley, not so", and he said: "She is dead upstairs. Go and see her." I went to his back door, and he followed me. I hesitated and did not go in. He passed me, and went into the back kitchen, and picked up a tableknife from a table behind the door. He then wiped it on a cloth. I went and told Mrs. Whitby and Mrs. Smith, and they both came to the house with me at once. He was still in the kitchen with the knife in his hand. I had not seen him previously that day. He did not seem any the worse for drink, and I noticed nothing peculiar about him.

Does that mean that it was normal for him to wander around clad only in a shirt?

Mary Anne Whitby: I am the wife of Septimus Whitby, of Number two, Hatton Park Road. About a quarter to four yesterday, I went with Mrs. Spriggs and Mrs. Smith to Wheatley's house. He was then standing behind the washhouse door, with only his shirt on. I noticed that his face was bleeding. I said: "Mr. Wheatley, have you cut your wife's throat?" He said: "I am sure I have'nt". Mrs. Smith said: "What have you done?" and he replied: "Nothing." I asked him whether we should go upstairs, and he said: "If you please, ma'am, do so." Mrs. Smith and I then went upstairs, and in the back bedroom, I saw Mrs. Wheatley, lying on the bed, close to the window. She was fully dressed. No bedclothes were over her. She was quite dead. She was lying on her back, with her head on the pillow. Her mouth was wide open. Her left arm was stretched straight out, and her right arm was bent so that her hand was close to her shoulder. Her legs were drawn up. I saw blood on the sheet near her left arm. Coroner: Was there a pillow or a scarf?

Mary Whitby: I saw only one pillow, and I didn't notice a scarf. Mrs. Smith and I then went downstairs. I said to Wheatley: "What have you done this for?" He said: "I was urged to do it. We are both done for, and they will hang me." I replied: "You must expect that." I also said: "I must fetch a policeman", and he said: "Do what you please, ma'am". I gave an alarm, and the people assembled outside the house. William Tomlin was one of the first to come up. When we left the house, Wheatley locked the door, and people weren't able to get in. The doors at the back and the front were locked. Soon afterwards, Dr. Clark arrived, and Wheatley opened the front door. Noone had gone into the house after I left, till the Doctor came.

Coroner: Do you know if the Wheatleys had quarrelled?

Mary Whitby: I have known Wheatley from his marriage eight or nine years ago. From what I have seen, I should say they were very unhappy nearly all the time. They frequently quarrelled. As late as last Saturday and Sunday, he turned her out of doors. He has frequently been the worse for drink lately. When he spoke to me yesterday, he appeared quite calm.

Coroner: Did he complain of being assaulted by his wife?

Mary Whitby: He did not.

Hannah Smith: I am the wife of Thomas Smith, of 3 Hatton Park Road. About a quarter to four on Tuesday, after what Mrs. Spriggs told me, I went with Mrs. Whitby to Wheatley's house. I saw him standing in the centre of the back kitchen, with nothing on but his shirt, and holding a tableknife in his hand. He wiped it with a cloth and put it in a table drawer. He wiped some blood off his face with the cloth. I said: "Mr. Wheatley, what have you done? Have you cut your wife's throat?" He said: "No, I am sure I haven't". Mrs. Whitby asked if we might go upstairs, and he said: "If you please, ma'am." He was very calm. I went upstairs with Mrs. Whitby, and we found Mrs. Wheatley lying on the bed in the back bedroom. I didn't examine the body, but I did what Mrs. Whitby said, and went down and said to Wheatley: "Mr. Wheatley, your wife is dead. I will go for the doctor and the police." He said: "If you please." I then went and informed Dr. Clark and a policeman.

Coroner: Were you aware of any quarrel?

Hannah Smith: I have known the Wheatleys ever since they were married. They had frequent quarrels. On Saturday, he turned her out of doors; and on Sunday afternoon, I saw her sitting outside the house on a chair. He came out and tried to lift her from the chair by her neck and her heels, as if to carry her into the house. In the struggle, the chair fell from under her, and she fell on to the path. I went towards them, and Wheatley went into the house. I never heard him threaten her, but she told me what a wretched life she was leading.

Robert Branch: I am a gardener. I reside at 7 Hatton Park Road. At ten minutes to two on Tuesday, I went home to dinner. Mrs. Wheatley came to my house and said her husband wanted to see me. I went to their house and took a lettuce with me. I asked him if he would like to have some salad, and he replied: "No, I don't want anything to eat". I then went home and made some salad, and took it to him. Mrs. Wheatley lent me a spoon and I said: "Open your mouth", and I fed him from the salad. He didn't seem to be ill, but Mrs. Wheatley said he wouldn't have a bit of anything to eat. They had some beans and bacon. He then said to me: "My dogs have been on your onions. What damage have they done? I will pay you for it." I said: "Oh, let it drop. I don't wish for anything." He then said to his wife: "You shouldn't have let the dogs out." She said: "You told me to let them out." He said: "You're a liar". I reproved him for using such language, and he said no more. I then went to get my dinner. He seemed a little excited, and he had the appearance of having been drinking. There was some fluid like beer in a glass on his table.

Coroner: Are you aware of quarrelling between them?

Branch: I hadn't seen him since last Friday. I have known them both for eight years, and I have known them quarrel occasionally, but only mildly. I have never heard him threaten her, but on Sunday afternoon, she was locked out with the children. At ten minutes to three on Tuesday, after I'd had my dinner, I returned to my work. He shouted to me as I passed his house: "Mr. Branch, my wife is drunk. Go upstairs and see her." I replied: "I cannot go up. My time is up, but I hope she will soon be better." He made no further remark, and that was all that took place.

Superintendent Bailie: What state was she in when you saw her?

Branch: She seemed to be sober.

A juryman: Did she make any reply when he called her a liar?

Branch: No.

A juryman: Was she sober when she fetched you to their house?

Branch: She appeared quite sober. As far as I know she was always sober.

A juryman: Did you see any scratches on Wheatley's face when you saw him at ten to three?

Branch: I did not, and I am sure he had none when I fed him the salad. Mrs. Wheatley said he had not been dressed that day, and he wouldn't put his things on, nor eat anything.

The next witness lived on the main road just round the corner from Wheatley's house.

William Tomlin: I live at 23 Harrowden Road. When I heard what happened, I went to Wheatley's house, about five minutes to four in the afternoon. I looked through the back window, and saw Wheatley come from the passage into the back room. He had a knife in his hand. I said to him: "Wheatley, what's the matter?" He made no answer, but waved his hand not the one with the knife. I asked him to unlock the back door, but he went to the front part of the house without answering me. I went round to the front window, and when Wheatley came into the room, a man who was standing near the window opened it. I said: "What's the matter?" He said: "My wife's dead." I said: "I hope that's not true." He said: "It's too true." I asked him to unlock the door and let some neighbours go and see, and he said: "No. No one shall come in this house today." He then went into the back room, while I waited outside till Dr. Clark came about ten minutes. Dr. Clark asked Wheatley to open the door, and he did so, and I followed the doctor in. Wheatley still had the knife in his hand. He didn't threaten us with it. He didn't speak at all. Dr. Clark took hold of his hand, and I took hold of the knife. He resisted me taking the knife away, and said: "No one shall have it", but it was taken away by three of us, Dr. Clark, myself, and a man named Maddison. Wheatley had nothing on but a shirt, and there was blood on his face. I have known the Wheatleys for a number of years, and they lived together very unhappily. I have heard them quarrel frequently. Before Tuesday, I saw him last on Sunday evening, when he appeared to have had a lot of beer. He was walking on the Harrowden Road, and he said: "Good evening." Mrs. Wheatley was a sober woman, but he'd been on the drink ever since last Easter, more or less. At the house, I went upstairs, but she was not in the room they usually slept in. His daughter works with me, and she fetched him twelve pints of beer on Monday.

Coroner: That evidence cannot be accepted. It is only based on hearsay.

Tomlin: I do not think he was sober on the Tuesday. I have known him threaten his wife.

Coroner: Have you heard those threats yourself? We cannot accept mere hearsay evidence.

The pathological evidence was heard next.

Dr. W. W. Clark: I am a medical practitioner at Wellingborough. About four o'clock on Tuesday, I was sent for to Wheatley's house in Hatton Park Road. I went to the front of the house and saw Wheatley standing within the front parlour window, which was open. He had a small tableknife in his left hand, and wore only a shirt. I asked him to open the front door, and he did so. I went in, followed by Tomlin. Wheatley stood in the passage. I asked him to give up the knife, but he said: "You shan't have it." He was excited, and one could see that he'd been drinking a great deal. I at once seized his left wrist, and with the assistance of Tomlin and others, the knife was taken away from him. There was no blood on it, but it had been freshly sharpened. He was excited in manner, no doubt from the after effects of drinking, bordering on delirium tremens. He had abrasions and scratches on his face, recently done, and bleeding. His nose had also recently bled. Having put him in the charge of several men, I went upstairs. In the back room, I found the deceased, lying upon her back, on the bed near the window, quite dead. She was fully dressed, and wore a cape pinned with a shawl pin, as if she had begun to dress to go out. I saw a hat lying on another bed. A small netted scarf [produced for the jury to see] was lying, rolled up, across the front of her throat. It had a litle blood upon it. The lips were livid, and her eyeballs rather prominent. There was no blood or froth about the mouth or nostrils, nor any marks of violence about her head or neck. I found blood on the back of her left hand, but there was no wound. A few drops of blood were upon the sheet at the side of her head, and the pillowcase was also stained. Later the same day, I made a post mortem examination of the body, in the company of Mr. A. Lloyd Perkins, and the only external mark of violence was an old bruise on the left shin. On opening the body, we found an effusion of dark venous blood under the right breast, which might have been caused by external pressure. We found the lungs were adherent on both sides, and very congested. The latter resulted, I believe, from suffocation. The heart was fairly healthy. The liver, kidneys and other organs were healthy. There was a little fluid in the stomach which had no odour. There were no bruises or extravasion of blood under the scalp, and no fracture of the skull. The brain was healthy, but very congested. The vertebrae of the neck were not fractured, and no bone of the body was broken. My opinion was that asphyxia was the cause of death, which might have resulted from pressure upon the chest. The lungs being adherent, and the deceased having a weak chest, she might easily have suffocated. I do not think the woman had been drinking heavily, either recently or at any other time. I saw Wheatley this morning, and I was of opinion that he was suffering from delirium tremens. I believe this to be the case on Tuesday, when I first saw him; and that was why I took the knife away from him, for it was impossible to tell what he would do with it. I think it is probable that he intended cutting his own throat. The deceased had been dead about an hour when I first saw her. I am quite of the opinion she did not die from natural causes.

Dr. A. Lloyd Perkins testified that he had assisted in the post mortem examination, and agreed with what Dr. Clark had stated. "In my opinion, death was caused by asphyxia, and not from natural causes."

Finally, the police evidence was heard.

Superintendent Bailie: ...From information I received from Mrs. Smith, I went to Wheatley's house on Tuesday afternoon. I found him in the kitchen, in the charge of William Tomlin and others, with nothing on but his shirt. Inspector Phenix took charge of him, and I then went upstairs, where Dr. Clark was examining the body of the deceased. After speaking to Dr. Clark, I went down and said to Wheatley: "Do you know your wife is dead?" He said: "Yes". I then said: "You may consider yourself in custody, on suspicion of having caused her death." In reply, he said: "Yes, all right. I will go with you." I then had him dressed, and sent to the Police Station. His face was bleeding, and I had it washed before sending him. He was certainly suffering from the effects of drink, but he understood what I was talking about. I took possession of the sheet, pillow and scarf. I know Wheatley has been drinking heavily of late.

Coroner, summing up: The question to be decided is: who was the cause of Mary Wheatley's death? The medical testimony shows beyond a doubt that the woman did not die from natural causes. There seems to have been only one person present, and we are driven to the conclusion that the husband caused her death. I believe, to shorten the story, that this will be the decision of your deliberations. Then again, you have to say whether he killed his wife with malice and without provocation, or whether he did it with such provocation as to reduce the charge from murder to manslaughter. Now there is no evidence of provocation whatsoever; or, if any, it is on the part of the accused, who called his wife a liar. The witness Robert Branch said that the deceased made no reply that she was quiet, and did not quarrel then. That being so, I do not think there has been sufficient provocation on the part of the deceased to justify you in saying that the accused is guilty of manslaughter and not murder. Shortly afterwards, the witness Branch was told by the accused, who at that time appeared to have no scratch upon his face, that his wife was upstairs, drunk. During this same afternoon, you have heard, the accused went out into the back yard with scratches and blood upon his face, and told the female witnesses that his wife was dead upstairs. With such circumstantial evidence before you, I think you will have little doubt in saying that the deceased met her death at the hands of her husband, and in the absence of any sufficient provocation, I am afraid you will be driven to find a verdict of wilful murder against John Wheatley.

The room was cleared. The jury deliberated for twenty minutes, and then announced their verdict: Wilful Murder by John Wheatley.

The commital proceedings took place at Wellingborough Police Court on Friday 31st July 1885, before two of the Magistrates, Woolston and Sharman. The Chief Constable of the County was also present. Wheatley was allowed to remain seated in the dock. During the evidence, he muttered several times, and was frequently reproved by his solicitor, Heygate, and by police officers.

The same witnesses gave the same evidence as at the Inquest. During the testimony of Mrs. Whitby about the position of the body,

Wheatley interrupted: "I pushed her back like that." He made a jerky action.

There was a new witness, a neighbour who had not been at the Inquest.

James Sears: I am a blacksmith, of 5 Hatton Park Road... Wheatley was drunk and quarrelsome on Saturday and Sunday. On Sunday afternoon, he fastened his wife out of doors. I lent her a piece of iron to open the door, but he took it off her, and put her outside again. After being out of doors some time, Mrs. Wheatley said she must go in to make her children's tea, and she went in. Soon after, she came outside with a chair, and while she was sitting on it, he came out and lifted her out of the chair and threw it at her. About eleven o'clock, Sunday night, I was outside my house, and I saw Wheatley and his wife. He called me a baby. I told him he ought to be ashamed of himself, and he said: "You ought to know better than to act so to the children." He then used a foul word to his wife, and said: "You are nothing but a bloody baby, and I'll make you a bigger one yet." He was drunk.

Heygate, crossexamining on behalf of Wheatley: Did the chair hit the deceased when the prisoner threw it at her?

Sears: I don't think so.

At this point, Wheatley, sitting in the dock, seemed to see something in front of him. He raised his fist at it, muttering, again.

The Chairman, C. J. K. Woolston, formally committed him to stand trial at the next Assizes. He was reluctant to leave the dock. "My cat's under the chair", he said, and bent down to search the floor space. Two policemen stood by as he began to dust the seat of the chair with his elbow. Finally he was grabbed and forcibly removed.

During the next few days, the London broadsheet appeared for sale on the streets: "SHOCKING WIFE MURDER..." Its subtitle proclaimed: "A man named Wheatley is committed for trial on the charge of murdering his wife. Drink is supposed to be the cause of the murder".

The Winter Assizes were held in Bedford on Saturday, 24th October 1885, before Lord Justice Denman. John Wheatley, charged with murder, and an alternative charge of manslaughter, was defended by Richard Harris, a barrister instructed by his solicitor, Heygate. Wheatley's manner was very quiet as he pleaded "Not Guilty". He was again allowed to remain seated in the dock.

Horace Smith (prosecuting): My Lord, this is a distressing case, seeing that the prisoner had borne an excellent character up to the time of this occurrence. I have no doubt that my friend, Mr. Harris, will be able to satisfy the jury as to his excellent character. For some reason or other, the prisoner became addicted to drink, and I shall prove by several witnesses that this was the cause of his quarrelling with his wife... I think I shall be able to show that death occurred from suffocation by a shawl, and violent pressure upon the chest.

The neighbours, James Sears, Robert Branch, Jane Spriggs, Mary Ann Whitby, Hannah Smith and William Tomlin, all testified as at the Inquest. Superintendent Bailie gave his evidence, and then, under cross-examination, added: "There was no blood on her face. There were two pillows on the bed. The bedclothes were not disarranged, except at the top. She was fully dressed. One of her knees was drawn up three or four inches; the other not so much. The room was 16 feet by 8 feet, and there were two beds in it.

Horace Smith, re-examining: Superintendent, you have described the back bedroom. Was that room used by the prisoner and his Wife?

Bailie: They slept in the front bedroom.

Judge: What caused the blood?

Bailie: Scratches, my lord.

In order to understand how the Bedford jury's perception of the case changed dramatically, we need to pay attention to the pathological evidence as presented at the trial. Dr. William Clark gave his version as before; but then he came under cross-examination by Richard Harris for the defence.

Harris: You took the brain out?

Dr. Clark: I did.

Harris: Was there extravasion of blood at the base of the brain?

Clark: There was not.

Harris: Is that not a normal accompaniment of suffocation?

Clark: It is usual, but there was none.

Harris: Have you ever known a case of death by suffocation without blood and froth coming from the mouth?

Clark: Never before. There were no traces of it here.

Harris: Did you notice the fatty state of the heart?

Clark: I did. There had been something wrong with the heart for some time, but I did not consider there was sufficient disease of the heart to cause death on extra excitement, nor that the deceased should have died from heart disease before she could have succombed to asphyxia.

Harris: Could not heart disease account for the congested state of the lungs?

Clark: Not in my opinion.

Horace Smith, reexamining for the prosecution: You say you have never before seen a case of suffocation without the aftereffect of blood in the mouth. Does that mean that such cases would not occur?

Clark: I have heard of such cases and read of them.

The Defence Counsel, Harris, would appear to have been taking medical advice. Indeed, he had. The Defence solicitor, James Heygate, had a kinsman, Frederick Heygate, with a medical practice in Wellingborough. Dr. Heygate was to be the only defence witness. He was now sworn.

Heygate: I am Frederick Nicholas Heygate, surgeon, of Silver Street, Wellingborough.

Harris: In your opinion, would a case of suffocation result in blood in the mouth?

Heygate: In cases of suffocation which have come under my notice, invariably I have found an effusion of blood from the mouth and nostrils.

Harris: I believe you knew the deceased Mary Wheatley as a Patient?

Heygate: I have known the deceased woman from about two years since. I attended her then for an acute attack of bronchitis, and I found that she had disease of the lungs of long standing, emphysema, and pleurisy; and she was also suffering from heart Disease.

Smith, cross-examining: Doctor, in two years, she was not affected by those symptoms.

Heygate: Two years ago, the disease of the heart was dangerous, and I then cautioned her against overexertion, which I was afraid would result in the sudden failure of the heart's action.

Smith: When did you see her last?

Heygate: I have not seen her since March of last year.

Smith: You did not see her after her death?

Heygate: I examined the body, especially the heart, on July 31st, at the request of the solicitor for the defence. I found that the heart had much more than a normal amount of fat on the surface. It was soft, flabby and pale, indicating fatty degeneration. I think it highly improbable, barely possible, that the deceased could have died from asphyxia, with her heart in the condition it was. Looking at all the postmortem symptoms I found, I consider that death arose from a shock acting on a weak, diseased heart. If she had died of asphyxia or smothering, I would have expected to have found venous blood at the base of the brain and there was none.

Harris, reexamining: Would it be possible to suffocate a woman with the small shawl we have seen?

Heygate: I think it would be very difficult to produce suffocation with that shawl, but it would depend on the power with which, and the manner in which it was held over the face, and the pressure on the chest. The latter forms a very material circumstance in cases of suffocation.

Richard Harris addressed the jury, obviously making much of his authoritative and contradictory medical testimony. The Judge, in summing up, pointed out that if the woman's death was materially produced by unlawful violence. on the part of the prisoner, even though she might have had heart disease and that was the immediate cause of death, then the prisoner would be guilty of manslaughter, not of murder, unless he intended to kill her.

The jury was out for half an hour. The verdict was "Not Guilty on either count". Wheatley was discharged.

"Shep" Wheatley returned to Wellingborough, followed by crowds, some cheering, some hissing.

A LAZY CARPENTER (1904)

On Tuesday, 15th March 1904, Samuel Rowledge went to a Northampton pawnbroker and took his revolver out of hock. Later in the day he shot his fiancee dead.

Sam lived with his 80 year old mother at 29 Chaucer Street, Kingsley Park, Northampton. He was an unemployed carpenter, aged 37. A popular distortion of the events, is that he and Alice Foster became engaged that very day, returned to the house and quarrelled. Not so. Alice was a domestic servant in Northampton, though her parents lived at Eastcote. The couple had been engaged for nearly a year, and Alice had spent much of the day looking for a suitable house for them to rent. Sam had called on his brother Alfred in Cloutsham Street. Alfred had offered him some work, fitting shelving in a customer's house, expecting that he would be glad of the money. When Alfred came home that evening, he was mystified to find that Sam had not been to do the work. The woman at the house was annoyed, having waited in for him.

Alfred walked to his mother's house. She was out, but Sam and Alice were there. Alfred demanded to know why the work had not been done. Alice was surprised. "You told me you had been and done it, she said to Sam. "You are lazy and deceitful."

Sam quietly walked out of the room and went upstairs. He returned directly, holding his revolver. It will never be known whether the first shot was aimed at Alice or at Alfred. They were both in the line of fire. Alfred dodged and scrambled through the door, as a bullet whizzed by his head. In the street, he heard a scream and two more shots. A man from next door went into the house and saw Sam near the body of Alice. "You can come in," said Sam, putting the revolver into his pocket. "I shan't hurt you." A policeman arrived, and arrested Sam who offered no resistance. At the Central Police Station, Samuel Rowledge was charged with the murder of Alice Foster, and the attempted murder of his brother, Alfred Rowledge.

The next day, at Northampton Guildhall, Rowledge sat below the Court while the Quarter Sessions took place. When all business was over, he was brought up before the Mayor, E. Lewis, and two other magistrates. His appearance was impressive, though he wore no shirt collar and tie. He was a tall man, with a heavy drooping moustache. He wore a tight black jacket, and seemed unaware that its collar was turned up. The Mayor read the first charge to him: "That he did wilfully and maliciously, and of malice aforethought, kill and murder one Alice Foster, in the house, 29 Chaucer Street, Northampton, by shooting her in the head and breast with a revolver, at 7.15 p.m. on Tuesday, 15th March 1904." The second charge was not read. Rowledge was remanded to the following Tuesday.

The same afternoon, C. C. Becke, the Borough Coroner, opened and then adjourned the Inquest on Alice Foster. She was 32 years old, one of a family of thirteen. She had been in service at Harrow, and then at Brigstock in the household of the noteworthy Vicar, the Rev. J. P. Sandlands. Most recently, she had been in service in Kingsley Park until giving notice a month previously, to prepare for her approaching marriage. Her body lay in the mortuary, with a powder scorched right eye and left breast, and was identified by her father, William Foster. The jury was bound over in the sum of £5 to attend the adjourned Inquest the following week.

On the following Tuesday, both the Inquest and the Commital Proceedings were completed. The Inquest jury found that Alice had been wilfully murdered by Samuel; and the Mayor sent him for trial at the next Assizes.

Justice Bray, a newly appointed judge, presided over the Northampton Summer Assizes. The trial of Samuel Rowledge began at 1.30 p.m. on Wednesday, 22nd June 1904. The Judge was seen to be carrying the black cap, and he placed it in front of him on the bench. Many clergymen were seen to be present in the crowded Court, and a large number of colourfully attired females had crammed themselves into the Grand Jury's gallery.

When the charge was put to him by the Clerk of the Assizes, Rowledge pleaded Guilty, but Mr. Stinson, a barrister appointed by the Court to defend him, whispered advice which resulted in a change of plea to "Not Guilty". Rowledge, wearing a dark grey suit, black tie and standup collar, (and carefully brushed moustache), watched the jurymen individually sworn.

William Gibbins, of the Northampton Borough Engineer's Office,produced a plan of 29 Chaucer Street.

William Foster: I live at Eastcote. I am the father of the deceased woman. She was aged 32 years, a domestic servant. She was engaged to Samuel Rowledge for eleven months. They seemed very fond of one another. On the 14th of March, the couple were at my house. They left early on the Monday morning, and that was the last I saw of my daughter. Their marriage was close at hand.

Suddenly, Rowledge, in the dock, disappeared from sight. He had bowed his head down onto his knees.

Elizabeth Rowledge: I am the wife of Alfred Rowledge. I am the prisoner's sister-in-law. At about nine o'clock, on the morning of 15th March, he came to see about an odd job my husband had got for him to do. He told me he was in a fix. I asked if I could help him, but he said I couldn't. I asked if Alice had come with him. She hadn't. He seemed very worried – said he thought the best thing he could do was to put a bullet through Alice, and himself too. I said, "That's nonsense to talk like that." I didn't think he meant it.

Stinson, cross-examining: What was his state of mind?

Mrs. Rowledge: I knew he had been out of work for six months or so. He seemed to be in a very worried state of mind.

Alfred Rowledge: I am the brother of the prisoner. I am a carpenter and joiner. Samuel was with me on Tuesday, 15th March. I gave him a job to do that afternoon, and he promised faithfully it should be done. When I found he hadn't been to do it, I went to see him in the evening. He was in the kitchen with Alice. I asked why he hadn't been to do the work. I said, "It doesn't seem as if you want any work." Alice said, "You must be lazy. You told me you'd been to work this afternoon." Sam turned to me and mumbled something, I couldn't understand. Then he left the room and went along the passage. I walked to the other door of the room. Alice was standing against the table. In a moment, Sam came back. He had a revolver in his hand, and he pointed it straight at me. It went off. I thought he was firing at me, though Alice was in a straight line between me and him. I ran out into the garden, and got over into the nextdoor neighbour's garden. I turned round to see if he was following me. I heard another shot, and then another. I told Mr. Wooding, who lives next door, and then went for the police. When I returned, the police were there, and Sam was handcuffed.

W. A. Metcalfe, prosecuting: Did your brother often quarrel with his fiancee?

Alfred: I never heard Samuel quarrel with Alice.

Mr. Stinson, cross-examining: There has been some mental illness in your family. Is it true that your mother's father was put under restraint for some years?

Alfred: I believe so; and she had a sister who died in an asylum.

Stinson: The trouble seems to have been caused by your brother's failure to do some work. Can you explain that?

Alfred: Mr brother had an injury to his right hand, which made it difficult for him to get employment. Alice was a bit nettled that he had not been to work. The shooting was so sudden, there was no time to get Alice out, and I didn't think he would harm her. I thought his resentment was towards me, not her. I thought she was in no danger from him.

Judge: Had your wife told you he had talked of putting a bullet through Alice?

Alfred: Not until I got home after this happened.

Stinson: Is it true that the prisoner had his head split open by a beam?

Alfred: Four years ago, yes.

Metcalf, reexamining: What made you believe he was likely to harm you, and not Miss Foster?

Alfred: He had threatened me several times.

Metcalf: When the beam fell on him, was his brain injured?

Alfred: I never heard of any injury to the brain.

James Wooding: I live next door to the prisoner and his mother. After the occurrence, I went into the kitchen, but I couldn't see anyone. I shouted, and Sam Rowledge jumped up from under the table.

Rowledge in the dock, sprang to his feet and called out: "That's a lie, sir. A barefaced lie."

Wooding: He was leaning over the body of the girl, and I said: "What's the matter, Sam?" He said: "Come in. I won't do you any harm." But then he pulled out the revolver from his pocket. He put his finger on the trigger and pointed it at me.

Rowledge, from the dock: It's a lie.

Wooding: It is not.

Rowledge: It is, sir.

Wooding: I said: "Stop a minute, Sam. We'll see about it. There'll be someone else here, shortly."

John Henry Haxley: I am the manager of a pawnbroker's shop in Northampton. Up to the 15th of March, the prisoner had a spirit level and a revolver in pledge with us, since July, 1903. On the 15th of March, he came in and pledged a coat and a watch for four shillings; and he redeemed the revolver and spirit level. He repledged the spirit level, and took the gun away with him. I remarked, as a joke: "Will she go? You're not going to shoot yourself, are you?" I was just making the remark to pass the time away.

Dr. James Beattie: I am Medical Officer of Health, and Police Surgeon, in Northampton. I was called to the house by the police. The woman appeared to have been dead a few minutes. There was a wound over the left breast. The clothes surrounding the bullethole were blackened with powder. That must have been an absolutely fatal wound. The second wound was from the right eyebrow, extending to the temple, and the skin surrounding this was blackened, so that the pistol had apparently been held close to the head. The wound might have been fatal by shock immediately, but in any case it would have eventually proved fatal from inflammation of the brain. The bullet had lodged in the left jawbone. At the mortuary, I found a third wound at the back of the neck, and the bullet had lodged in the spinal Cord.

Police Constable Chamberlain, Northampton Borough Police: ...On the night in question, I was at home in Byron Street. I was called to the house in Chaucer Street. From the front, I could see the prisoner in the back kitchen. He was lying prostrate on the body of the young woman. I went through the nextdoor neighbour's to the rear of the house. He was still in the same position. I tried the door, but I couldn't open it, and at that moment, P.C. Mallard arrived. The prisoner called out: "Who's there?" He came to the door. He then left the door and went across to the fireplace. He lit a pipe, and sat down by the fire. To get in, we had to push the feet of the body away from the door. We then rushed in and took the revolver from his left trousers pocket, and handcuffed the prisoner. He said: "You can come in. I aren't agoing to do any more." The brother came in and said: "I should like to say, gentlemen, that he shot at me first." To which the prisoner instantly replied: "You're a liar. I did not."

P.C. Mallard: ...When charged, the prisoner said: "That's right, but I did not do it with any malice or illfeeling. That's altogether wrong." To a charge of attempting to murder Alfred Rowledge, he replied: "That's a lie. He was outside the door before I fired a shot."

Inspector Collings: The revolver is a six chambered one. There was a cartridge in each chamber, three of which had been fired. The bullets corresponded with those in the body of the deceased. At the prisoner's request, I went to him in his cell. He said: "The revolver will prove whether I fired at him. There are three cartridges fired, and three wounds in the girl." At that time, we only knew of two wounds. The prisoner said: "There are two wounds in the head and one in the breast; and three left. So how could I fire at him?" I said: "That is the statement he has made." To this, he replied: "It is a lie, and that proves him a liar." There was blood on the prisoner's left hand.

Lee F. Cogan: I am Medical Officer at His Majesty's Prison, Northampton. The prisoner has been under my observation. I examined him carefully, with regard to his mental state, and found no deficiency and no signs of mental unsoundness whatever. I am aware of the old injury to his head.

Stinson, cross-examining: Should you have been surprised if he had committed suicide?

Cogan: He might have done.

Stinson: You think he is a person who might?

Cogan: I have no reason for supposing he has suicidal tendencies.

Stinson: You don't think he was serious when he said, "I must put a bullet through Alice and myself as well."

Cogan: I don't look upon him as a person of suicidal tendencies. I don't attach importance to that statement.

Stinson: Do you think him a person likely to do a rash act without any reasonable motive?

Cogan: I look upon him as a sane man, and therefore one who would not do an unreasonable act.

Metcalf, re-examining: Would you consider that every person who committed a rash act without reasonable motive, was mad?

Cogan: No, I should not.

Metcalf to the Judge: That ends the case for the Crown. I ask the Jury to say that the prisoner was perfectly sound in mind when he committed the act.

Mr. Stinson addressed the jury, eloquently, on Rowledge's behalf. "...It is for you, the jury, to say whether he is to meet an ignominious death, and whether his name is to be indelibly stamped as a murderer. You are probably taking part in the most solemn duty of your lives. The pity of it all is that it need not have happened if the brother had shown a little more pluck and presence of mind, and reasoned calmly with him... The man's mind was unhinged for that moment. There is an entire absence of motive for the crime. I desire that He to whom all hearts are open and from whom nothing is hid, might direct you Aright.

Judge Bray, summing up: ...The responsibility on you is great, but you must not hesitate to discharge your duty, even if the evidence compels you to find him guilty... With regard to the question of motive, you have not got to find that, at that moment, he had some ill will towards the girl. It was for the prosecution to prove that he killed her, and for the defence to prove by affirmative evidence that he was insane not by merely negativing the medical evidence. In order to find him insane, you must be satisfied that he did not know what he was

118

doing, that he did not know what shooting her with a gun would do, or if he did, that he did not know he was doing wrong...

The Judge then entered into a detailed review of the evidence. He made clear his attitude in regard to suggested insanity: "The evidence of insanity is of the vaguest possible description, and cannot be relied upon. The doctor regards him as a sane man."

At 1.20 p.m. the Jury went out. The Judge left the Bench, and the crowd in Court began to chatter, unrestrainedly and very loud. At 1.37, the Jury returned, and almost at the same time, the Judge returned. There was utter silence.

Clerk of the Assizes: Gentlemen, have you agreed upon your Verdict?

Foreman: We have.

Clerk: How say you? Is the prisoner at the bar guilty or not Guilty?

Foreman: Guilty.

Clerk: You say he is guilty of the crime of wilful murder.

He turned to Rowledge, and his voice broke with emotion: "Samuel Rowledge, you are arraigned on a charge of wilful murder, and on that arraignment you have thrown yourself upon your country. You have been found guilty of the crime of wilful murder. Have you anything to say why sentence should not be pronounced on you, and why you should not die according to law?

The Judge's Marshal placed the black cap on Judge Bray's Head.

Judge: Samuel Rowledge, the jury have found you guilty, on evidence which can leave no doubt, of the crime of murder. I have only one duty to perform, and that is to pass sentence that you be taken hence to the place of execution, and that you be there hanged by the neck until you be dead, and that your body be buried within the precincts of the prison in which you were last confined...

Sam Rowledge spent the next twenty days in the large cell on the southeast corner of the yard of Northampton Gaol, watched by relays of two warders. The law required three clear Sundays to elapse before the sentence was carried out. The fatal day should have been Tuesday, 12th July, but William Billington, the Executioner, was not free on that day, and the hanging was postponed until Wednesday. Billington, and his assistant, Henry Pierrepoint, were lodged in the Gaol overnight. They were given a choice of ropes by the Under Sheriff of the County, and allowed to watch Rowledge walking in the exercise yard, to enable them to judge the length of the drop. The scaffold was tested with bags of sand.

The execution shed was a plain wooden building. The scaffold was on ground level, so that no steps needed to be climbed. It comprised a great oaken beam, one foot square, supported by two uprights. A new hempen rope dangled over the trap door.

On Wednesday morning, 13th July, 1904, Sam Rowledge was awakened and given a light breakfast at seven. Billington and Pierrepoint went into the cell and pinioned his hands high behind his back. At five minutes to eight, a mournful procession began from the door of the cell. The Chaplain led, reading portions of the Burial Service. The Governor, Lieutenant Lionel Sanders, R.N., followed; then the Under Sheriff, the Surgeon (Lee Cogan), and Rowledge supported by two warders. Billington and the Chief Warder, Broxton, brought up the rear. The route across the yard was covered by a white cloth, so that it was out of the sight of other prisoners and the houses opposite the wall.

It was a bright, sunny morning. The tolling of the bell of the nearby Church of Holy Sepulchre; the murmur of the large crowd outside the gate, and the reading of the Chaplain, were the only sounds.

As soon as they were inside the shed, Billington adroitly strapped Sam's legs and pulled a white cap over his head. He swiftly adjusted the rope, and pulled the lever. Some in the crowd outside distinctly heard the lever and the clank of the heavy trap door.

Sam Rowledge swung for one hour, and then he was taken down and laid out on a table in the shed. At ten, C. C. Becke, the Borough Coroner opened the Inquest, with a jury of thirteen. The jurymen viewed the body. The rope marks were plainly visible, and the face had turned green. Governor Sanders began the formal evidence: "I am the Governor of His Majesty's Prison, Northampton. The deceased, Samuel Rowledge, first came here on March 16th on remand. He was a carpenter by occupation, and his age is stated to be thirty seven years. He was charged with wilful murder, and was duly tried and convicted at the last Assizes and sentenced to be hanged, which sentence was duly carried out this morning at 8 o'clock."

Under Sheriff: I am Henry William Kennedy Markham, Under Sheriff for the County of Northampton. On behalf of the Sheriff, I received the warrant for execution which I now produce, and which was duly carried out this morning.

Lee Cogan: I am Surgeon to His Majesty's Gaol. I was present at the execution this morning. It was properly carried out and death was instantaneous.

Coroner: The law directs that, since executions have taken place in private, a coroner's jury shall inquire to ascertain if everything was properly carried out. You have heard the evidence, and will have no difficulty in coming to the conclusion that the body viewed by you, was the identical body of the said offender, and that the said offender was a male person of the age of 37 years and a carpenter.

Foreman: We find that this execution was carried out in due course of law.

The verdict was signed by C. C. Becke and posted outside the gates.

There was a break with tradition. The black flag was not hoisted over the gates.